Conway Moncure Daniel

Travels in South Kensington

With Notes on Decorative Art and Architecture in England

Conway Moncure Daniel

Travels in South Kensington
With Notes on Decorative Art and Architecture in England

ISBN/EAN: 9783337345570

Printed in Europe, USA, Canada, Australia, Japan

Cover: Foto ©Andreas Hilbeck / pixelio.de

More available books at **www.hansebooks.com**

Travels

IN

South Kensington

WITH

Notes on Decorative Art and Architecture in England

BY

MONCURE DANIEL CONWAY

AUTHOR OF
"THE SACRED ANTHOLOGY," "THE WANDERING JEW," "THOMAS CARLYLE," ETC.

ILLUSTRATED

LONDON
TRÜBNER & CO., LUDGATE HILL
1882
[*All rights reserved*]

THE SOUTH KENSINGTON MUSEUM

DECORATIVE ART AND ARCHITECTURE IN ENGLAND

BEDFORD PARK

CONTENTS.

	PAGE
THE SOUTH KENSINGTON MUSEUM	19
DECORATIVE ART AND ARCHITECTURE IN ENGLAND .	115
BEDFORD PARK .	215

ILLUSTRATIONS.

	PAGE
The Statue of His Royal Highness the Prince Consort . . . . *Frontispiece*	
South Kensington Museum . . .	21
Sir Henry Cole, K.C.B.	36
South Kensington Museum — Ground Plan	39
Diagram showing Glitter Points in a Picture-gallery	40
Sir Philip Cunliffe Owen, Director of South Kensington Museum . . .	42
North Court, North-west Corner, Showing Casts of the Biga (or Two-horse Chariot), from the Original in Marble at the Vatican, and of the Pulpit by Giovani Pisano, formerly in the Cathedral at Pisa	44
South Court, Showing the Prince Consort's Gallery	45
Chinese Potters at Work — Window in the Ceramic Gallery	47
Italian Majolica (Urbino). Sixteenth Century	51
Lamp from an Arabian Mosque. Fourteenth Century	53
Palissy, the Potter — Window in the Ceramic Gallery	54
Sèvres Porcelain Vase. Modern . .	55
Henri Deux Candlestick	56
Henri Deux Salt-cellar	58
Michael Angelo's Eros	62
Marble Cantoria. By Baccio D'Agnolo	65
Tabernacle. Andrea Ferrucci . .	66
Altar-piece — the Virgin with the Infant Saviour. — Enamelled Terra-cotta, or Della Robbia, in High Relief. By Andrea Della Robbia	67

	PAGE
Hercules, the Duke of Ferrara . . .	70
Ashantee Relics	72
The Cellini Sardonyx Ewer, Mounted in Enamelled Gold, and Set with Gems — Italian. Sixteenth Century . . .	73
Châsse, or Reliquary — Limoges Enamelled. Thirteenth Century . . .	75
Pastoral Staves — Ivory and Enamel. Fourteenth Century	82
Elkington's Mark	85
Franchi and Son's Mark	85
Modern Persian Ewer (Copper-coated, with White Metal)	94
Old Persian Earthenware (Water-bottle)	95
Persian Kaliân	96
Ancient Persian Incense-burner (Pierced and Chased Brass)	97
Modern Persian Incense-burner (Brass)	98
Andrea Gritti, Doge of Venice — Italian. Ascribed to Vittore Camelo. Sixteenth Century	99
Tazza — Algerian Onyx and Enamel. Modern French	100
Salt-cellar — Silver Gilt; Italian. Fifteenth Century	100
Ivory Tankard — Augsburg. Seventeenth Century	101
Finest Raised Venetian Point Lace — Floral Design. Italian. Seventeenth Century	104
Nettle in its Natural State	109
Nettle in Geometrical Proportions . .	109
Plan of Top of Henri Deux Salt-cellar .	111
Assize Court, Manchester	122
Minton Tile	124

	PAGE		PAGE
Kidderminster Carpet—Fern Design	127	Moulding over Dado	186
Minton Tiles for Mantel	129	Chippendale Mahogany Moulding, Belmont House	187
Albert Memorial, Hyde Park	131	Drawing-room of Bellevue House	188
Albert Memorial. Europe	133	Library in Bellevue House	191
Albert Memorial—East Front. Painters	134	Drawing-room in Townsend House	194
Albert Memorial—Continuation of East Front. Painters	136	A Grate of One Hundred Years Ago	198
		Grate made for Baron Rothschild	199
Albert Memorial—South Front. Poets and Musicians	138	Boyd's Grate	200
		L. Alma Tadema.—[From a Bust by J. Dalou]	207
Albert Memorial—Continuation of South Front. Musicians	140	Candelabra, Townsend House	209
Spandrel Picture	147	View from a Balcony	217
Owen Jones	153	Dining-room in Tower House	222
Ebony Serving-table, Mr. Lehmann's House	162	Queen Anne's Gardens	224
		Co-operative Stores and Tabard Inn	225
Top of Serving-table, Mr. Lehmann's House	164	Tower House and Lawn-tennis Grounds	226
		Reading and Billiard Room, Club-house	227
Pot Designed by Miss Lévin	167	A Fancy-dress party at the Club	229
William Morris	185	An Artist's Studio	233

PROLEGOMENA.

HOMELY and Comely were sisters. Their parents were in humble circumstances, and depended mainly on the care and economy of these two daughters—their entire family. They were persons of some social position, and it had constituted a problem how they might preserve some relation to the community and at the same time maintain comfort at home: Youth required the former, Age needed the latter. It was settled in a way which this historian cannot commend: the arrangement was that one of the girls should attend to the external, the other to the internal affairs of the family. So soon as this was resolved, there was no difficulty in determining which of the girls should go out and which stay at home. There was about Comely a certain ease and address, as well as personal attractiveness, which seemed to make society her natural sphere; while the shyness and plainness of Homely made the task of remaining at home congenial. Homely was content with homespun clothes in order that Comely might wear silk. Whenever there was a ball or a festival, Comely was sure to come, and Homely stayed at home.

Gradually, however, this distribution of parts appeared not to have the happiest results. Comely grew so fond of the gay world that her home became distasteful; she demanded, too, more and more of the family resources for her fashionable attire, and the concession deprived the house of everything but the barest utensils. On the other hand, Homely had stayed within-doors so much that she became slovenly, and, as she had to wear her homespun till it was threadbare, in order that her sister might keep up with the fashions, she became unlovely to look upon. Comely came at length to despise her sister. Homely became a peevish drudge. The family by degrees became unhappy, without being very clear as to the cause of their troubles.

One night Comely came home from a ball in unusual agitation. Her sister was aroused to hear the confidence that a lover of rank, handsome and charming, had discovered his interest in Comely. Any differences the sisters may have had were quite forgotten in the renewal of their natural sympathy caused by this incident.

The next morning a messenger arrived to announce that his master, Lord Deeplooke, was on his way to visit Comely and the family in their own home, and would arrive in an hour. Here was a sensation! The two sisters set themselves to work—even Comely using her hands for once—to make the chief room of the house neat. But Comely looked on the blank walls with dismay, and said, "Surely there used to be some pictures." "Yes," replied Homely, "but you are wearing the last of them now." Comely blushed—and the blush was becoming—at this; but the sisters gathered some beautiful flowers and decorated the room as well as they could. When this was attended to Comely was about to repair to her room to decorate herself, and called her sister to do the same; but Homely declared she already had on her very best gown. Comely was shocked at this, and entreated her sister to conceal herself during the nobleman's visit. This Homely was quite willing to do.

When Lord Deeplooke arrived, Comely met him in the finest array she had next to the ball-dress. She introduced him to her venerable parents; but a shade of anxiety passed over her face when she observed his lordship presently looking around as if he expected some one else. She then remembered that the messenger had announced that he was coming to visit not her alone but the family, and that on the evening before, at the ball, she had casually mentioned her sister. With a quick wit Comely anticipated the inquiry she knew would be made and left the room, remarking, as she did so, "I pray your lordship to excuse me while I seek my sister." Another moment and the two girls were hurriedly investing Homely in Comely's second-best dress.

It was a novel experience for Homely to be dressed in a pretty gown; it was equally novel for her to be introduced to a gentleman, much less a lord; and the two novelties together had an almost transforming effect upon her. Home-work and early hours had kept her in perfect health; her manners had no chance to be other than simple; and as no experiences of fashionable life had made her *blasé*, her face was suffused with an exquisite color, and her eye bright with delight, when she entered the room and was introduced to his lordship.

The reader must not be kept in suspense for another instant. It was not Comely but Homely that Lord Deeplooke ultimately married. Homely having discovered the secret that lay in a becoming dress, chiefly from its effect on the feeling of the wearer, stoutly refused to be slovenly any more; and all her serviceable virtues, thus set in a fit frame, were found to have touched her countenance into unconventional beauty. On the other hand, Comely, though at first jealous and angry, gradually appreciated the lesson she had been taught. She did not, indeed, forget the magical effect wrought on her sister by a beautiful dress; but she pondered deeply the qualities fostered at home which she had supposed incongruous with such raiment, but now saw particularly harmonious with it; and thenceforth, even before Homely was married, Comely devoted herself to household work. Need I say that in this Comely was far more successful than her sister had been? All the beauty she had seen in the gay world, an occasional visit to which she still enjoyed, now became available. Pictures reappeared on the walls, which her sister had supposed were just as useful without them. Touches of color, a ribbon on the curtain which had hitherto been tied with a string, a hundred refinements which required only a cultured taste, gradually transformed the house, just as Comely's dress had transformed Homely. For these improvements Comely had been glad to part with her mere finery, though she never forgot that a slovenly mistress makes a slatternly home.

Comely subsequently married an artist, who, beginning life as a sign-painter, was made a knight for the best example of domestic decoration exhibited at the Great Exposition of 18—, a model which, he frankly confessed, was suggested by the house in which he found his bride.

There are, indeed, few words in our language of more peculiar, or even pathetic, import than the word "homely." It has gradually come to bear the significance of coarseness or even ugliness, as if these were quite appropriate to the home. It is, indeed, fortunate that the home can supply affection for things and persons not very presentable; but it is none the less true that the word has gradually come to represent the impression that beauty is for outside show, and that anything will do for home purposes.

Decoration (*decus*) means the bestowal of honor. Beauty followed honor. Because man honored his deity, grand temples and cathedrals arose and altars blazed with gems; and because he honored the prince and the noble, palaces were decked with splendor. All this time the home remained homely, for religion denied its sanctity and aristocracy despised it as the dwelling-place of a serf. The wealthy called their residences palaces, châteaux, castles, villas, seats, anything but "homes." The "Home" came to mean some common asylum of the poor. But at last two mighty forces invaded Europe — Democracy and Heresy. Sternly they forbade man longer to spend his strength and his honor on allied Tyranny and Superstition. Then the Arts declined, because the convictions which had inspired them were shaken. Several of the grandest cathedrals were struck by a sort of paralysis and could never get finished, and palaces had to continue their grandeur on terra-cotta and tinsel.

And now the cunning workman, having struck work upon shrines and thrones, began to think of his own mind, so long left vacant that temples might be adorned, of his wife and child, so long stinted that palaces might be luxurious. The first expression of this new reflection was not outward: it was in the decoration of men's minds with furniture of another kind—with science, poetry, and literature. Enamored of these deeper pleasures, man almost despised and hated the outward arts which symbolized his long thraldom. And perhaps it was necessary that the ancient splendors which invested a departed era should fade, and that man should retire as into an ugly shell to mature the pearl of an inner life. The old artists, artisans, potters— the Bellinis, Angelos, Palissys, Della Robbias — reappeared in Rousseau, Milton, Bunyan — artists of an invisible beauty, disowning Art while frescoing the mind with ideals.

For a time the work of imagination went on in humble dwellings amidst Puritan plainness. But finally, even in the beginning of this generation, it began to be asked in England whether the mind and heart thus formed might not be honored with a fit environment of beauty. To this end London established its great School of Design and Decoration. Thereto have gravitated the fragments of a Past that has crumbled—images, altars, shrines, decorations lavished by genius on ideals ere they hardened to idols; imperial services, jewels, sceptres, wrought before kings became survivals and phantasms. It is England, land of beautiful homes, reviving the art of decoration for the Age of Humanity. She will no longer have the home to be homely. Her call has gone round the world, and temples and palaces deliver up their treasures that they may gather in London, there to teach the millions how they may beautify the latter-day temple, which is the Home, and refine the latter-day king, which is Man.

It is said that the Londoner may be known, in any part of the world where he may die, if his lungs are examined—they being of a sooty color. So much of his great metropolis he is doomed to carry with him wherever he may journey. London itself must forever bear, through and through, the effect of its fogs and its climate. Rain was its architect and Smoke its decorator. But let no one hastily conclude that their work has been all unlovely. John Ruskin has pointed it out as a characteristic of the greatest English artist, Turner, that there was nothing so ugly about England but he could bring beauty out of it; but that fine artist, Necessity, worked long before Turner in transmuting apparent disadvantages to advantages. "It is," said Charles Kingsley, "the hard gray English climate which has made hard gray Englishmen." There is as little *terra-cotta* on the Englishman's house as on his character. It has been determined for him by Rain and Fog that he shall seek his pleasures by the fireside instead of in public gardens and fêtes. What beauty he can afford must be of the interior. Without, gray dirty brick and wall; within, every comfort and refinement: such are the decree of his superficially dismal decorators. Of course the wealthy Londoners have always fought against their hard climatic environment, and against the ever-encroaching ugliness which is the attendant shadow of millions massed together in the struggle for existence on a small island. There are still a few mansions, only a little way from the present centre of London, which attest the fine taste which its wealthy citizens have always tried to cultivate in the direction of architectural beauty. About two hundred and fifty years ago Northumberland House was described as "in the village of Charing." That is now Charing Cross, the heart of the metropolis; a street runs over the site of Northumberland House. Where once was Charing hermitage is now a huge hotel and railway station. About two hundred years ago, when the Earl of Burlington was building Burlington House on Piccadilly, about half a mile west of Charing Cross, he was asked why he was building so far away in the country, and replied, "I am resolved to have no house beyond me." The earl's resolution was not kept. He lived to find himself amidst a noisy thoroughfare, and now one may travel five miles to the westward of his old country-seat without leaving the avenue of brick and mortar which passes its door. This migration of dwellings to ever-extending suburbs is, indeed, traced in much grander buildings than the tasteful old mansions which are being swallowed up because of their uneconomical occupancy of space: so much general stateliness is secured by the vast increase and diffusion of wealth; but the rarity with which the unique beauties of the older mansions are imitated, and the utter absence of any attempt at individuality in even the wealthiest new quarters—such as Belgrave Square—would seem to indicate that the Londoners have finally adopted it as a creed that external architecture and gardens must no longer be sought for by individuals, but possessed by all in communal forms, as public edifices, squares, and parks. It is now usual, in the new parts of London, for the grandest mansions of a terrace to own a large garden in common, to which each has entrance by a back gate, and to whose maintenance and ornamentation each family contributes a small sum per annum.

In its journey of eighteen centuries, from being that small trading-village mentioned by Tacitus—"not yet dignified with the name of colony"—to its present dimensions, covering 125 square miles, London has been formed by forces of use, by world-historical movements—powers not to be criticised. But we may admire in some of the characteristics of its mighty growth some of that beauty which ever works at the heart of the hardest utility. For example, in its expansion London is said to have swallowed up and built over more than three hundred villages; but in every case the village-green has been spared, and these are now represented by those beautiful and embowered squares which everywhere adorn the metropolis, constitute with the seven large parks its lungs, and make it the healthiest city of the world in proportion to its population. Though the ancient houses built by the wealthy were beautiful, and, wherever remaining, bring such large prices that one wonders why they should not be imitated, yet the homes of the lower classes in old times were far uglier than now. Especially were they made dismal by that barbarous "tax on light," whose monuments may frequently be observed in windows walled up to avoid the window-tax. The poor had to live in houses illuminated from one or two windows, until the clever gentlemen of the Exchequer perceived the costliness of this means of revenue. As the Swiss mountaineers have come to admire goitres, unless belied by rumor, and as the city man, from having to put up with "high" game, has gradually come to prefer it, so the London builders for a long time placed few windows in houses, and seem to have thought the effect solid and "English," as contrasted with the light and airy style of French houses. The newest streets of London show, however, that light on this subject has dawned upon the English architectural mind, through that into the homes of the people, to such an extent that the tax is now upon darkness. It is now accepted as a principle that as Smoke has had its way with the outside of the London habitation, hereafter the first decorator of the interior is to be—Light.

In these fragmentary first pages of a fragmentary work, it has been the author's aim to outline certain general ideas and historical facts, which may illustrate their own illustrations as written in the following pages. It will be best seen, when approached from the historical side, what may be regarded as a necessary factor in English art or architecture, and what may be considered as experiment. This is the more important for the American, who is, in an especial sense, "heir of all the ages," while not limited to the grooves prescribed by any. It is in America that we are to have the great Art of Arts—that whose task is to utilize the Arts of other lands and ages as pigments, to be combined into new proportions for unprecedented effects, and to invest fairer ideals. For America the author has written these contributions toward a knowledge of what has been done, and is being done, in England; but he would prefer now to burn his work rather than have it aid the retrogressive notion that Art in America is to copy the ornamentation or duplicate the work of other countries, much less of other ages. These things can mean for the artists and people of the United States nothing more than culture; and culture means not a mere eclectic importation of select facts and truths, but their recombination, in obedience to a new vital principle related to a further idea and wider purpose.

THE SOUTH KENSINGTON MUSEUM.

SOUTH KENSINGTON MUSEUM.

THE SOUTH KENSINGTON MUSEUM.

"COME," said my friend, Professor Omnium, one clear morning, "let us take an excursion round the world!" My friend is a German, and he has such a calm familiarity with the unconditioned and the impossible, that a suggestion which, coming from another, would appear astounding, from him appears normal. This time, however, I look through his spectacles to see if his eyes have not a merry twinkle: they are quite serene. Visions of the Parisian play entitled *Round the World in Eighty Days*, thoughts of Puck and excursion tickets, rise before me, and I gravely pronounce the word "Impossible!"

"But," says the professor, "Kant declares that it is too bold for any man, in the present state of our knowledge, to pronounce that word."

"My dear friend," said I, "it is among my dreams one day

to visit India, China, Japan, California; but at present you might as well ask me to go with you to the moon."

"You misunderstand," replies Professor Omnium: "I do not propose to leave London. We can never go round the world, except in a small limited way, if we leave London. How much does an excursionist in India see of that country? Only a few cities, a few ruins, and the outside of some old temples, and he only sees a little of them. I stayed in Rome three days once—all the time I had there—trying to get a glimpse of some antiquarian treasures in the Bocca della Verita Church: first day, the church was closed to all outsiders by regulation; second day, the building was occupied by a pious crowd, and services were going on from daybreak to midnight; third day was so dark and rainy that I couldn't see anything. On my way back I met an archæologist who had been in Nuremberg a week trying to scrutinize an old shrine; he had seen many priests, but only caught glimpses through railings of the shrine (St. Sebald's, which exists in full-sized fac-simile at South Kensington), and the net result of his journey was represented in fifty photographs, just a little inferior to my own collection of the same —bought in Regent Street. I tell you, sir, there are few greater humbugs than this travelling about to see Objects (with a big O) of Interest. It's expensive. Somebody says most travellers carry ruins to ruins, but the purses they carry away are the worst ruins of all. A man may well travel to see the world of men and women; but so far as art and antiquity are concerned, he who goes away from London shall have the experience of the boy in the fable, who dreamed about the beautiful blue hills on the horizon until he left his own flinty hill-side and journeyed to them; he found them flintier than his own, and, looking back, saw his own hill to be bluest after all."

"Ah, then," I put in—when Omnium is talking it is well to put in when one can—"you begin by asking me to go round the world, and end with sneering at all my dreams of India and Japan—"

"Not a bit of it," cried the professor; "but ten thousand

people and a dozen governments have been at infinite pains and expense to bring the cream of the East and of the West to your own doors: you turn your back, and pine for the skim-milk. Yesterday I was talking with Dr. Downingrue, an amiable and learned gentleman, who has been an official in the India House here for twenty years, and was lately given furlough for a year. That year he passed in Turkey and Persia. He told me that he wished to see a certain sacred book, written in ancient Zend, curiously illustrated with the most ancient pictures in the world, one of them possibly a portrait of the great Zoroaster himself. It was, he had heard, kept in the archives of the city of Bam Buzel, and he went a journey of three days and nights in a wagon to see and examine its text. Fancy his disgust at finding only an entry that the volume in question had been removed by order of the Shah in 1855, and that the Keeper of the Archives knew nothing whatever of its whereabouts. I took Downingrue by the hand, led him up one flight of stairs, and took down the old Zend book from its shelf there in Downing Street, where it had remained quietly, twenty feet over his head, while he worked twenty years for freedom to go searching for it in Persia! Now I heard you talking a few evenings ago about your hopes of one day seeing Shiraz and Mecca, the Topes in India, and the great Daiboots Buddha in Japan. I have called this morning to say, firstly, Don't! secondly, Come, go round the world with me here in London! There is in the South Kensington Museum as noble a Buddha as that at Daiboots, which hundreds of thousands of pilgrims have journeyed for weeks to see: you have only to walk fifteen minutes to see it—not a copy either, but the huge bronze itself. You may travel through Mexico, Peru, and Chili for ten years, and in all that time never see one-hundredth part of the vestiges of their primitive life and history which you shall see in the British Museum. Greece?—and be captured by brigands. Professor Newton has Greece under lock and key, from Diana's Temple to the private accounts of Pericles. Assyria?—you go, and find that the human heart of it has migrated; you come back, and George Smith reconstructs it for you—"

There was no sign that Omnium was ever coming to an end: the only way of stopping him is surrender; and it was not long before we were making our pilgrimage through Stone Age and Bronze Age, as recovered by the ages of Iron and Gold, and still more by the ages of Art and Science. The professor held a very positive theory that to travel round the world profitably you must first travel up to it, assimilating its past ages. Two recent stories had taken a strong hold on his imagination: one was about a learned historian of his own Germany, who had resolved that it was essential to the complete culture of his little son that the child should begin where the world began, believe implicitly in its fetiches, follow them till they changed to anthropomorphic gods and goddesses, these again till the Christian wand transformed them to fairies and demons, and so on. By this means the historian meant that his boy should bear in his individual periods of life corresponding periods in the growth of the race, and sum up at last the long column in a total of rational philosophy; but the boy is now growing old, and at last accounts had got only as far as Roman Catholicism, and there—stuck! The other story which haunted Omnium's mind came from California, and was to the effect that upon the head of a woman in mesmeric sleep there was laid the fossil tooth of a mammoth, whereupon she at once gave as graphic a description of the world the extinct animal had inhabited when alive as could have been given by any paleontologist. "Both good stories, eh?" said the professor, with a hearty laugh; "almost as good as Pilpay's fables: both of them fictitious notions ending in fantasies; but both, so to speak, prophetic types of what real science with real materials enables us to do to-day. We can, indeed, 'interview' the mammoth, as you Americans say; we can hang his portrait on our walls along with our other ancestors; and we can assimilate the education of the human race, not by beginning with being assimilated by its embryonic ages, risking failure to pick through the egg-shell at last, but by bringing to bear the lens of imagination, polished by science, and carrying so a cultured human vision through all the buried City of Forms."

Since the few mornings when I had the pleasure of rambling with my German friend in the museums of London, and listening to his raptures, I have passed a great deal of time in those institutions, and with a growing sense that his enthusiasm was not misplaced. Indeed, so far as the museum at South Kensington is concerned—to which the present paper is especially devoted—to study it with care, and then stand in it intelligently, must, one would say, convey to any man a sense of his own eternity. Vista upon vista! The eye never reaches the farthest end in the past from which humanity has toiled upward, its steps traced in fair victories over chaos, nor does it alight on any historic epoch not related to itself: the artist, artisan, scholar, each finds himself gathering out of the dust of ages successive chapters of his own spiritual biography. And even as he so lives the Past from which he came over again, he finds, at the converging point of these manifold lines of development, wings for his imagination, by which he passes on the aerial track of tendency, stretching his hours to ages, living already in the Golden Year. There is no other institution in which an hour seems at once so brief and so long. A few other European museums may surpass this in other specialties than its own; though, when the natural history collections of the British Museum are transferred to their magnificent abode at South Kensington, one will find at the door of this museum a collection of that kind not inferior to the best with which Agassiz and others have enriched the Swiss establishments; but no other has so well classified and so well lighted an equal variety and number of departments, and objects representing that which is its own specialty—Man, as expressed in the works that embody his heart and genius.

The museum has been in existence about twenty-five years (1882). Its buildings and contents have cost the nation about one million pounds: an auction on the premises to-day could not bring less than twenty millions. Such a disproportion between outlay and outcome has led some to regard South Kensington as a peculiarly fortunate institution; but there has been no luck in its history. Success, as Friar Bacon reminds us, is a flower that implies a soil of many virtues. If magnificent collections and invaluable separate donations have steadily streamed to this museum, so that its buildings are unceasingly expanding for their reception, it is because the law of such things is to seek such protection and fulfil such uses as individuals can rarely provide for them. I remarked once to a gentleman, who did as much as any other to establish this museum, that I had heard with pleasure of various American gentlemen inquiring about it, and considering whether such an institution might not exist in their own country, and he said: "Let them plant the thing and it can't help growing, and most likely beyond their powers—as it has been almost beyond ours—to keep up with it. What is wanted first of all is one or two good brains, with the means of erecting a good building on a piece of ground considerably larger than is required for that building. The good brains will be sure to recognize the fact that we have been doing a large part of their work for them at South Kensington. It is no longer a matter of opinion or of discussion how a building shall be constructed for the purpose of exhibiting pictures and other articles. The laws of it are as fixed as the multiplication table. Where there have been secured substantial, luminous galleries for exhibition, in a fire-proof building, and these are known to be carefully guarded by night and day, there can be no need to wait long for treasures to flow into it. Above all, let your men take care of the interior, and not set out with wasting their strength and money on external grandeur and decoration. The inward built up rightly, the outward will be added in due season."

There is no presumption in the high claims of the curators and architects of the South Kensington Museum for the principle and method of their building. For it must be borne in mind that every difficulty that could conceivably present itself had to be solved by them in its extreme form: they had to deal with the gloomiest and dampest climate and the smokiest city in the world, and, *a fortiori*, they have solved every difficulty that can arise under less dismal skies. Nevertheless, this museum need not rest upon the claims made in its behalf by any authority. No statement can be so instructive and impressive as its own history, so far as that history exists; for, great as is the success it has attained, there is no one aspect of it which, if examined, does not reveal that it is rapidly growing to a larger future. I applied to a man who sells photographs of such edifices for pictures of the main buildings. He had none. "What, no photograph of the South Kensington Museum!" I exclaimed, with some impatience. "Why, sir," replied the man, mildly, "you see, the museum doesn't stand still long enough to be photographed." And so, indeed, it seems; and this constant addition of new buildings, and of new decorations on those already erected, is the physiognomical expression of the rapid growth and expansion of the new intellectual and æsthetic epoch which called the institution into existence, and is through it gradually climbing to results which no man can foresee.

From a valuable paper on local archæological museums, contributed to the *Building News*, June 11th, 1875, I gather some of the following facts relating to the origin of the chief English museums. In the middle of the seventeenth century there was formed at Lambeth, in London, the first place that could be described as a museum. It was called "Tradescant's Ark." It consisted of objects of natural history collected in Barbary and other states by Tradescant, sometime gardener to Queen Elizabeth. This valuable collection was bequeathed, in 1662, by the younger Tradescant to Elias Ashmole, who gave it to Oxford in 1667, and it was the basis of the now valuable Ashmolean Museum of that place. Sir Robert Bruce Cotton, after graduation in 1585, associated with the antiquaries of his day, Joscelin, Lambard, Camden, and Noel, and collected rare books and antiquities, which became the nucleus of the British Museum. Sir Hans Sloane died one hundred and twenty years ago, and by will offered his collection of MSS. and artistic and natural curiosities (for which he had paid £50,000) to the nation for £20,000. In 1753 the Harleian collection was purchased. When a place in which to deposit these treasures was sought, Buckingham

House (now Buckingham Palace) was offered for £30,000; but an offer by Lord Halifax of Montague House (built by Hooke, the mathematician) for £10,000 was accepted, and so the museum stands at Bloomsbury. The public was first "admitted to view" (the phrase is still used at the museum) the collections in 1759. George II. presented the old Royal Library, founded by Henry VII., containing monastic spoils. The Lansdowne MSS. were bought in 1807 for £4925; the Burney collection, eleven years later, for £13,500; and in 1820 Sir J. Banks bequeathed his library of natural history. At the time of the foundation of the British Archæological Association in 1844 there were outside of London but three museums, namely, at Oxford, York, and Salisbury. Now nearly every large town has its museum in which to treasure the monumental relics and natural curiosities of its neighborhood. York has the sarcophagi, tessellated pavements, and altars of *Eboracum*, Salisbury the spoils of *Uriconium*, Colchester the remains of *Camulodunum*, Bath those of *Aquæ Solis*, and Cirencester those of *Corinium*. The Brown Museum at Liverpool is rich in Anglo-Saxon remains, and the important collection described by Wylie in his *Fairford Graves* is in the Ashmolean at Oxford. The Brown Museum derives its name from Sir W. Brown, who not only added to it a large building, but his collection (which cost him £50,000) of consular diptychs, Etruscan jewelry, Limoges enamels, Wedgwood pottery, and important Roman and Saxon antiquities. The Scarborough Museum has interesting British relics, among them a tree coffin of great rarity. The Exeter Museum has a good set of Celtic pottery, and bronze implements found in Devon. Wisbech possesses superb examples of mediæval art and important Egyptian antiquities. In the Torquay Museum may be found the vast collection of flint implements found in the famous Kent's Cavern through the industry of Mr. Pengelly, the geologist, along with remains of extinct animals discovered beside them. The Halifax Museum, in which Professor Tyndall passed his early scientific apprenticeship, is rich in the curiosities of the coal measures, and has important Egyptian as well as Roman remains. There are many other museums in the country—indeed, hardly any important town is without one; but I must not fail to mention a very interesting one at Canterbury. It contains Roman tessellated pavements; a large number of ancient terra-cotta forms, presented by the late Viscount Strangford, who brought them from the Greek isles, Egypt, and Asia Minor; two extremely interesting Runic stones found near Sandwich; and many such interesting antiquities as the "Curfew Bell" and "Couvre Feu;" and some very odd ones—for instance, the severed hand of Sir John Heydon, who was killed by Sir Robert Mansfield in a duel, anno 1600.

In a graphic article published some years ago Sir Henry Cole described (what it is almost impossible for the Londoner of to-day to realize) the condition of this metropolis at the beginning of the century. The only institution which then existed for preserving any object of art or science was the British Museum, which was founded in 1753, in which year a sum of £300,000 was raised by lottery to purchase certain collections—as that of Sir Hans Sloane, and the Cotton MSS.—over the drawing of which lottery (100,000 tickets at three pounds each), at Guildhall, the Lord Chancellor, the Speaker of the House of Commons, and the Archbishop of Canterbury presided! But this sole institution excited the very smallest interest in the country, and so late as forty years ago Croker jeered in Parliament at Bloomsbury as a *terra incognita*, and Carlyle's brilliant friend and pupil, Charles Buller, wrote an article describing a voyage of exploration he had made to that region, with some account of the curious manners and customs of the inhabitants. "About a hundred visitors a day on an average," says Sir Henry Cole (there are now as many visitors to the British Museum per hour)," in parties of five persons only, were admitted to gape at the unlabelled 'rarities and curiosities' deposited in Montague House. The state of things outside the British Museum was analogous. Westminster Abbey was closed except for divine service, and to show a closet of wax-work. Admittance to the public monuments in St. Paul's and other churches was irksome to obtain, and costly:

even the Tower of London could not be seen for less than six shillings. The private picture-galleries were most difficult of access, and, for those not belonging to the upper ten thousand, it might be a work of years to get a sight of the Grosvenor and Stafford collections. No national gallery existed, and Lord Liverpool's government refused to accept the pictures now at Dulwich, offered by Sir Francis Bourgeois, even on condition of merely housing them. The National Portrait Gallery, the South Kensington Museum, and the Geological Museum were not even conceived. Kew Gardens were shabby and neglected, and possessed no museum. Hampton Court Palace was shown, by a fee to the house-keeper, one day in the week. No public schools of art or science existed in the metropolis or the seats of manufacture. The Royal Academy had its annual exhibition on the first and second floors of Somerset House, in rooms now used by the Registrar-general, whose functions then had no existence. It was only at the British Institution or at Christie's auction-rooms that a youthful artist like Mulready could chance to see the work of an old master, as he has often told us. Dr. Birkbeck had not founded the present Mechanics' Institute in Southampton Buildings, and the first stone of the London University, in Gower Street, was not laid. Not a penny of the public taxes was devoted to national education. Hard drinking was as much a qualification for membership of the Dilettanti Society as the nominal one of a tour in Italy. Men's minds were more anxiously engaged with bread riots and corn laws, Thistlewood's conspiracy and Peterloo massacres, Catholic emancipation and rotten boroughs, than with the arts and sciences, for the advancement of which, in truth, there was hardly any liking, thought, or opportunity."

This being the condition of London, the state of things in other parts of the United Kingdom may easily be inferred. There are now fifteen important public museums and art galleries in or near London. The ancient buildings of interest are shown without fees. More than a million people visited a single one of these museums last year. There are seven large schools for art training in London alone, and 151 in the whole country, with 30,239 pupils. The number of pupils at South Kensington Art School for the scholastic year ending July, 1880, was 824. These numbers refer exclusively to those who mean to devote their lives to art. The official report for 1881 gives 4758 as the number of elementary schools in which art is taught, 768,661 as the number of children instructed, the total amount of the grants in aid of them being £43,203 in the same year.

Public interest in the treasures of art and science in London —whose extent was unknown to any one—first manifested itself in 1835, when Parliament caused an inquiry to be made into the state of the British Museum; a second committee inquired in 1847, a third in 1859. The result of these inquiries was a series of ponderous Blue-books, which few ever saw, but which that few studied very carefully. It finally burst upon the country that the British Museum and its collections had, up to 1860, cost three millions of pounds, and that it was "in hopeless confusion, valuable collections wholly hidden from the public, and great portions of others in danger of being destroyed by damp and neglect." The commissioners of 1859 who made this report also pointed out the cause of the evils they recognized. The museum was in the hands of forty-seven trustees, each of whom seemed to think that there were plenty to manage the affair without his concerning himself individually in the matter. Never was costlier broth so near being spoiled by multiplicity of cooks, when Panizzi, by a sort of *coup d'état*, brought a strong executive control to bear upon it. It is a singular fact that even now the British government does not formally adopt the British Museum. The vote for supplies of its ways and means is given each year on a motion made by a member sitting on the opposition benches. During Mr. Gladstone's administration it was made by the Right Hon. S. Walpole, a trustee of the museum; when Lord Beaconsfield was in power it was made by the Right Hon. Robert Lowe, also a trustee. The money is supplied grudgingly. There can hardly be found elsewhere men of such eminence in their own departments as Professor Newton, Reginald

Stuart Poole, and Story-Maskelyne (the mineralogist); there can be found none who have done such enormous work in bringing order out of chaos in the British Museum; yet they receive salaries of six hundred and fifty pounds each for labors that deserve a thousand. The condition of this museum has much improved of late. The vast growth of its collections had crowded its literary and scientific employés into miserable unventilated cells, and their murmurings of years have until now been unheeded. When the first victim, the Talmudic scholar, Emanuel Deutsch, was dying, he said, "Perhaps when I am gone they will do something." This was the hope of the thirty-eight scholars buried alive in the printed-book department. He died, and nothing was done. Then fell the second victim, Mr. Warren, head of the transcribing department. This caused a panic. The readers of the reading-room, many of whom suffer from the now medically recognized "Museum headache," took the matter up. The trustees visited the room where the two scholars had perished, and condemned it. But several rooms only a little better were still used, and another able assistant, an eminent author, barely saved his life by resigning a post he had held in the museum for over twenty years. The principal librarian, Bond, and keeper of printed books, Bullen, have done much to improve the state of things; but there is still a great want of private rooms for the assistant librarians, who generally have to sit in draughty galleries, where no open fires are to be got at. That this huge building should have become absurdly inadequate for its contents and its original purpose indicates the vast progress of English science in recent years. The keepers of antiquities felt themselves bound to declare that there were valuable Egyptian, Assyrian, and Greek monuments and inscriptions, in the crypts and corners of the museum, quite as useless for scientific purposes as if they had remained buried in the lands where they were exhumed. Much relief, both to the assistants and to the scholars who have had to dig like Schliemann for some of the museum's treasures, will follow the removal of the vast zoological collections to South Kensington. The final result will be that the British Museum will be specialized, and become the treasury of the national archives and the national library.

As for the matter of payment, it certainly constitutes the gravest problem besetting institutions of this character. The best work done for literature, art, and science (so far as they are connected with the state) is done on small salaries, a thousand pounds being considered a vast sum for great men. Even such men as Tyndall and Lockyer get less than that by their official positions. But these gentlemen all feel the danger that might arise if such work became so well paid as to allure the incompetent, and its offices become objects of political intrigue. At present no country is better served in such matters than England, such men as those mentioned being content with small salaries because of the ample means of research afforded them. And indeed it would appear enough to prevent the offices for scientific and other work of an intellectual character being sought for gain, if some clever statesman would invent a way of paying the additional sums needed "in kind," but in some kind, also, not transmutable into values for other than the learned. It must be admitted that thus far no English minister has appreciated the necessity that scholars should have salaries sufficiently large to raise them above anxiety, and to render unnecessary the too frequent frittering away of invaluable time and power in a multiplicity of extraneous and lucrative employments.

The redemption of the British Museum, so far as it has proceeded, as well as the establishment of nearly every institution of importance to art or science in the country, was largely due to the instruction by example represented in the South Kensington Museum. This institution, it is important to remember, did not grow out of any desire to heap curiosities together or to make any popular display: it grew out of a desire for industrial art culture, and the germ of it was the School of Design which opened in a room of Somerset House, June 1st, 1837. This poor little school is now a thing to make fun of. It took over a month for it to obtain the eight pupils with which it began. The first act of its regulators seems to have been a rule that "drawing the human figure shall *not* be taught to the students." Haydon insisted that there could be no training without the human figure. The government did not want artists, but men who could draw such patterns as should render it no longer necessary for English manufacturers to go to Lyons and Paris for such. Etty and Wilkie sat in the council beside silk-weavers and portly warehousemen. Fine-art students were actually excluded—this mainly because of the cry that the government would otherwise be taking bread out of the mouths of private teachers—and the School of Design in 1842 consisted of 178 pattern-drawers. Schools of a similar character were gradually established in some of the provincial manufacturing cities. And there had been about ten years of this sort of thing when the great Exhibition of 1851-52 took place.

Queen Victoria has described the May day when the Palace of Glass was opened in Hyde Park as the happiest of her life. She had witnessed one of those noble victories which leave no tears behind but such as may welcome glad tidings of good-will, and she had seen her hero wearing the only crown he coveted—that of success in a great achievement for European civilization. It is sad indeed that only as a widow does she live to realize the latest results of that day on her country.

The great Exhibition may be termed, so far as English art is concerned, the great revolution. Such a display of "florid and gorgeous tinsel," to use Redgrave's description, was never seen, unless in the realms of King Coffee. The articles from the Continent were glittering and showy enough, but those of Great Britain outglittered all, exciting the laughter of cultivated foreigners to such an extent that English gentlemen were scandalized and abashed without knowing precisely what was the matter. The Prince Consort, who was especially ashamed at the general disgust manifested for this tawdry English work, had brought with him from his careful training in Germany and at Brussels one excellent habit—that of deferring to the judgment of accomplished men in matters relating to their own specialties. When he found himself, as Chief Commissioner of the great Exhibition, the hero of a great æsthetic failure and of a great financial success—blushing for the fame of the country which had bestowed its highest honor upon him, and at the same time contemplating a net surplus of £170,000—the idea took possession of him that the least the money could do would be to begin the task of raising English work from the abyss of ugliness which had been so admirably disclosed; and that idea led him to consult artists of ability and men of taste, and to mediate between them and her Majesty's complacent ministers, whom he managed to rouse into a happy state of bewilderment, which resulted in action.

The Prince Consort was, during his brief life, a fortunate man in many respects, but in nothing was he so fortunate as when, inspired by the best artistic minds in England, he induced the Queen to set apart some rooms at Marlborough House (now the residence of the Prince of Wales) for an industrial art collection and for art training, and when he persuaded her ministers to devote £5000 to the same purpose. He has thus made the great head-quarters of British art in some sense his monument. In 1852 the small collection of the School of Design in Somerset House was removed to Marlborough House, and the Board of Trade confided to Owen Jones, R. Redgrave, and Lyon Playfair the work of reorganizing the whole art training of the country. The collection transferred from Somerset House was trifling enough, but now there were added a number of articles that had been purchased from the Exhibition, and a still more remarkable collection, which has a curious history. After the French Revolution, when the infuriated people were prepared to destroy not only the *noblesse*, but the works associated with them, fine cabinets and beautiful china vanished out of Paris. At this time George IV.'s French cook gathered up a superb collection of old Sèvres china. This had long been distributed through the English palaces, and was even used for ordinary table service; it was now, by the Queen's order, removed from the various palaces to Marlborough House, where it was at once recognized as the finest existing collection of a class of articles which was already exciting that competition among collectors which at present amounts to a mania. But the Queen's best loan was her example. Ministers took up the matter with unwonted courage. Mr. Henley, of the Board of Trade, secured the Bandinell pottery, Mr. Gladstone the Gherardini models, and the precedent was set which has since added the Bernal, Soulages, Soltikoff, Pourtalès, and other collections—one of the most curious being that of the Rev. Dr. Bock, a collection of mediæval religious vestments. There is a myth still current that in one or two cases the secret agent of the British Museum had been bidding for some treasure against the secret agent of South Kensington; but it has no foundation. Once upon a time the British Museum and the Tower of London found themselves bidding against each other for a piece of old armor; but no similar accident could have occurred under the keen eye of Sir Henry Cole, who from first to last has been felt in the progress of this museum. Sir Henry developed a power of getting money for the museum, from the stingiest chancellors, unknown in the history of the English exchequer. He, with Mr. Richard Redgrave, explored Italy, and brought back many valuable treasures of early art.

SIR HENRY COLE, K.C.B.

In 1854 the first report of the newly-established Department of Science and Art was laid before Parliament. It was a Bluebook of 642 pages—so much being required for those interests of the country to which the Board of Trade had, in 1836, devoted the half of one page. This report and those which followed bore witness that a new enthusiasm had arisen in England for recovering its lost arts; but they increasingly proved also that the collections evoked from their hiding-places were already overflowing Marlborough House. In one sense this overflowing was of signal advantage, for it enabled the department to send a collection of four hundred beautiful specimens as a circulating museum through the provincial cities and towns—a plan which has been maintained by the museum, and also by the National Gallery of Fine Arts, with excellent results. The commissioners had not at that time, so far as their reports show, any notion of localizing the various schools of science and art at South Kensington. Indeed, no such expression as "South Kensington" had existed until 1856, when Earl Granville so christened the "Brompton Boilers," which the government had empowered Mr. Cole to prepare for the transfer of the Marlborough House collection (voting £10,000 for the purpose), and which, with their three boiler-shaped tops, still stand as the seed-shell of the museum. It was little supposed then that the "Mr. Huxley" whom the report of 1856 speaks of as employed to collect specimens on the coast would ever be seated as he is now in a palatial science school at Kensington. There must, however, have been some very far-seeing eyes looking at things in those days, for the commissioners of the great Exhibition of 1851 persuaded the government to add to the Exhibition surplus of £170,000 enough to make £300,000, and to invest the sum in the vast Kensington Gore estate. This estate comprised between twenty-five and thirty acres of land, twelve of which belong to the museum, and has become the site of a great metropolis of science and art. The museum was opened on June 22d, 1857, by the Queen, accompanied by the Prince Consort and the Heir Apparent.

The removal of the collections of Marlborough House to South Kensington, and the establishment of the new movement in a centre of its own, with room to grow, was speedily followed by a grand event, namely, the donation by Mr. Sheepshanks of his superb collection of pictures to the nation. Mr. Sheepshanks supplies to gentlemen who wish to benefit the public about as good an example as they can find in modern annals. For many years he had welcomed artists to study and copy in the gallery opening from his dining-room, which so many of them now remember as an oasis in the wilderness which surrounded them in the last generation. But the owner of this gallery had observed that the Philistines of Parliament were still very strong: they had once refused to accept even a valuable collection of pictures (as already stated) from unwillingness to house them; and although they had got beyond that, and thankfully accepted the Vernon Gallery, he saw that the arrangements for giving shelter to this gallery were made very slowly. The National Gallery had a large portion of its Turner and its Vernon bequests housed at South Kensington, and a much larger portion of them hid away in its crypt, for twenty-five years, awaiting the hour when England should find out the magnificent works of which it is the heir, by seeing them on the new walls completed in 1876. Mr. Sheepshanks resolved to see his gallery—which was worth even then a hundred thousand pounds—attended to while he was yet alive. He offered his pictures to the country on the following conditions: that a suitable building should be erected at Kensington (which would remove them from the dust and smoke of the city); that they should never be sold; must be open to art students, and at times to the public; and that the public, especially the working-classes, should be permitted to view the same on Sunday afternoons. The government assented to all of these conditions except the last, and Mr. Sheepshanks was reluctantly compelled to add to that provision the words, "it being, however, understood that the exhibition of the collection on Sundays is not to be considered one of the conditions of my gift."

Having thus summed up the history of the museum, it remains for me to consider its three aspects: (1) as to architecture and decoration; (2) its collections of objects; (3) its educational or art training method and character.

The accompanying map will show the series of buildings at South Kensington. There exists to the west of Exhibition

Road a park of about ten acres, holding at the north the Royal Albert Hall, at the south the Museum of Natural History, and between these, on either side, the long line of arcade buildings containing the National Portrait Gallery, the Indian section, Naval Museum, Patent Office, the Museum of Scientific Apparatus, and, in addition, spacious halls for the display of machinery during exhibitions, for horticultural shows, and Mr. Frank Buckland's methods of pisciculture. Such a collection of museums,

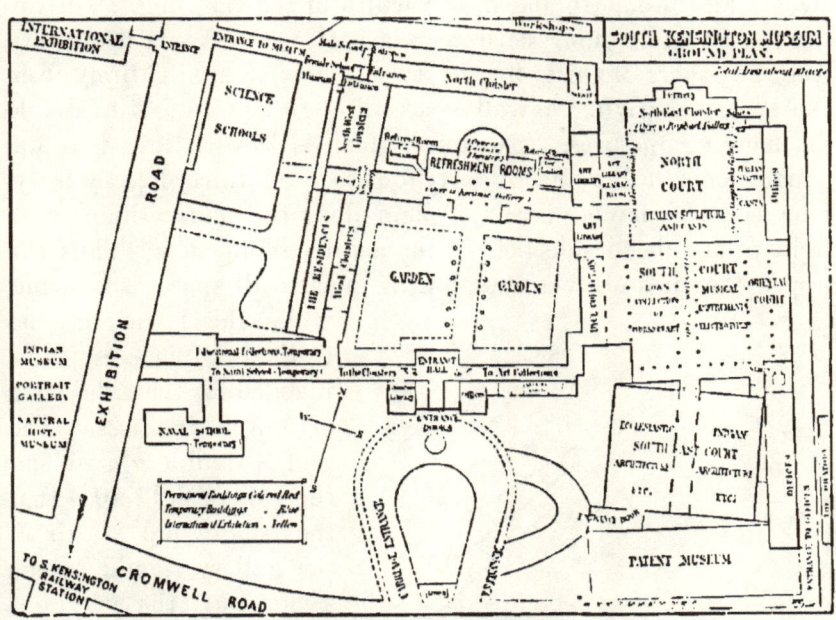

SOUTH KENSINGTON MUSEUM—GROUND PLAN.

answering the varied needs of science and art, cannot be found elsewhere — even within the limits of a nation. The gardens adjoining this series of buildings are beautifully adorned with statues and fountains, and will remain in the future, as they have been in the past, a favorite promenade, entered from Albert Hall and its extended galleries, in summer always bright with flowers, with music, and gay companies.

The building containing the courts was designed by the late

Captain Fowke, of the Royal Engineers, and, I believe, there is no other building in this country more adapted to its purpose. The task assigned Captain Fowke was to build a picture-gallery eighty-seven feet long by fifty wide, with two floors, the upper to be lighted from above, and the lower open to the light from side to side, and to make the whole as near fire-proof as possible. The building is thirty-four feet above the ground-line to the eaves, and fifty to the ridge, and consists of seven equal bays, twelve feet in length and of the width of the building. The upper floor contains four separate rooms, two of forty-six by twenty feet, the others of thirty-five by twenty feet, lighted entirely from the roof, and giving a wall space of 4840 square feet available for hanging pictures. The lower floor is thrown into two unequal rooms of forty-six by forty-four feet and thirty-five by forty-four feet, each having a row of piers along the centre, the play of light from side to side being thus nearly unimpeded. Thus the upper floor has no windows, but as much wall space as possible, while the lower has no walls, but piers, as is demanded for the exhibition of objects in cases. The roof is double glazed, and the rule of lighting is that the height and width of the gallery should be the same, and the skylight half of the same. This renders it always easy for the spectator to avoid the glitter point on a picture, as may be seen by the accompanying diagram.

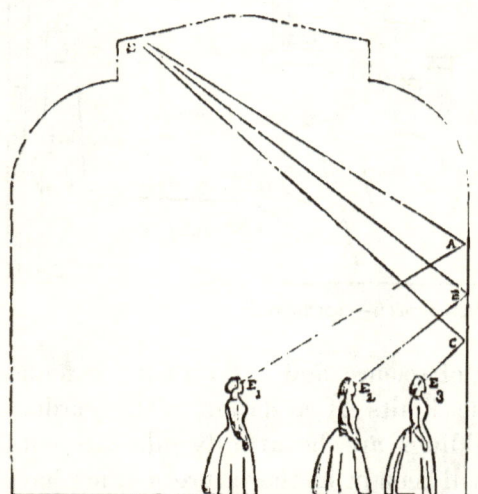
DIAGRAM SHOWING GLITTER POINTS IN A PICTURE-GALLERY.

The glitter point, altering with the position of the beholder, is at B, nine feet from the floor, when the beholder is at E_2, or five feet from the wall; and the glitter descends to C, seven feet from the floor, when the beholder advances to E_3. But if the spectator can recede to fifteen feet, the wall has no glitter up to thirteen feet. The skylight at South Kensington is brought as near as is consistent with avoiding glitter, and is twenty feet nine and a half inches from the floor. Just below the skylight run horizontal gas-pipes, with fish-tail burners projecting on two-inch brass elbows, and the light at night is as nearly as possible the same as in the day. When the gas was first put in this building there occurred an interesting controversy concerning the effect of gas on pictures, which elicited a valuable statement, jointly signed by Faraday, Hofmann, Tyndall, Redgrave, and Fowke, who had been appointed as a commission of inquiry, to the effect that coal-gas is innocuous as an illuminator of any pictures, if kept at a sufficient distance above them to avoid bringing into contact with the pictures the sulphuric acid caused by its combustion ($22\frac{1}{2}$ grains per 100 cubic feet of London gas).

In the large courts electric lamps are now used with much success. It is wonderful to note the beauty of porcelain and all objects of delicate decoration under the new light; it brings out the minute traceries better than daylight.

Security from fire here has been made as nearly absolute as possible, and Sir Philip Cunliffe Owen believes it impossible by any device to fire the museum; yet the water arrangements and vigilance at South Kensington are as complete as if the building were built of the ordinary materials. As a matter of fact, the choice of materials was made after long and patient scientific experiments. The main material is the best gray stock brick, with ornamental work of certain blue, red, and cream-colored bricks peculiar to some English counties. Some iron it was, of course, necessary to use for joists and girders, but in every case this iron has been isolated by being surrounded with a thick fire-proof concrete. The floor is of Minton tiles imbedded in Roman cement. The double roof is Mansard, and covered with a French tile (*tuile courtois*), selected at the Paris Exhibition of 1855.

THE SOUTH KENSINGTON MUSEUM.

The picture-gallery described above, made to hold the Sheepshanks collection, has had additions made behind it, in accordance with the original plan, of three large rooms, which contain various collections of pictures, and near the back entrance to these is the gallery of Raphael's cartoons. All this series of picture-galleries constitutes an upper floor of a wing to two vast

SIR PHILIP CUNLIFFE OWEN, DIRECTOR OF SOUTH KENSINGTON MUSEUM.

derble show-rooms. One of these is a large square apartment, in which large numbers of marble and other antique monuments are displayed. The other, connected with it, is architecturally divided by slender pillars—between which, as an avenue, are show-cases, above and below—into two noble rooms with splendid arched ceilings. The first-named of these rooms (that which is without division, and single-roofed) has not yet received its wall decorations, which are to be a distemper half-way up, and above, a frieze of frescoes large as Raphael's cartoons. The other show-room—with the double-arched ceiling—furnishes, as may be imagined, fine opportunities for wall decoration, as also for the ornamentation of floor and ceilings. The decoration here has not been completed, but it has gone far enough for the scheme to be judged by its effect.

And it is just here that a careful criticism is necessary. While the purely architectural work merits all the praise that can be claimed for it, securing an admirable play of light, making each division add its light to the other, and reducing the space occupied by pillars and other accessories to a minimum, the decorations are but measurably successful. The faults are due, I think, to the intention that the ornaments themselves should present some of the features of a collection of styles. The result proves that it would be better if the varied styles were exhibited in a court set apart for the purpose. The floor, for example, is rich in its varieties of tiles, there being some five or six of different designs and shades. It is true that the great central floors are made of tiles of uniform design and color, and that these—a deep brick red, with small green spots at the corners of each tile—are grave and good; but all around, where we pass through arch or door, there is a deep fringe of brilliant tiles, which are reflected into the glass cases nearest them, to the injury of the objects shown; and in the series of "cloisters," as the spaces beneath the picture-gallery may be called, there are further experiments in floor tiles which militate against the effect of the articles exhibited in them. The ceilings in these cloisters, or side spaces, have been covered with Oriental decorations by the late Owen Jones; they are Indian, Persian, moresque, and of the greatest beauty, each coffer in the ceiling and each archway presenting a new design, and yet all in harmony: these being too far above the show-cases to affect any objects in them, are rightly placed; but the floor, as the necessary background to many objects in the rooms—many of which depend on delicate shades of color for their effect—will eventually, I suspect, have to be reconstructed, and made entirely of the grave hue which has happily been already adopted for the greater part of it. Ascending a little above the floor, it must be said also that there is too much brilliancy about the lower arches and their spandrels—too much white and gold. It is not only that this does not give a sufficiently subdued background for the bright glass or chased metals in the upper parts of the cases (on the ground-floor), but they are by no means the best supports for the grand series of life-sized figures in mosaic, on deep gold surfaces, which make the magnificent frieze of the upper wall.

NORTH COURT, NORTH-WEST CORNER, SHOWING CASTS OF THE BIGA (OR TWO-HORSE CHARIOT), FROM THE ORIGINAL IN MARBLE AT THE VATICAN, AND OF THE PULPIT BY GIOVANI PISANO, FORMERLY IN THE CATHEDRAL AT PISA.

It is these superb figures, representing the great artists of the past, which constitute the most salient feature of decoration in the museum. In this case (as in so many others in the museum) the scheme—due to the late Mr. Godfrey Sykes—of combining the purposes of general decoration with subjects of special interest in a museum, has been most fortunate: the general effect is noble, the figures interesting as portraits and as representations of costume, the varieties of mosaic in which they are produced being of value for comparison. There are thirty-six flat alcoves —eighteen on each side—and the figures in them are those of the chief artists in ornamentation, with the names of their designers beneath: Phidias (by Poynter); Apelles (Poynter); Nicola Pisano (Leighton); Cimabue (Leighton); Torel, the English goldsmith, d. 1300 (Burchett); William of Wykeham, bishop and architect of Winchester Cathedral, d. 1404 (Burchett); Fra Angelico (Cope); Ghiberti (Wehnert); Donatello (Redgrave); Gozzoli, one of whose Florentine frescoes, containing his own portrait, is in the museum, d. 1478 (E. Armitage); Luca della Robbia, specimens of whose terra-cotta work in the museum show him to have been a man of genius, d. 1481 (Moody); Mantegna (Pickersgill); Giorgione (Prinsep); Giacomo da Ulma, friar at Bologna and painter on glass, d. 1517 (Westlake); Leonardo da Vinci (J. Tenniel); Raphael (G. Sykes); Torrigiano (Yeames); A. Dürer (Thomas); P. Vischer (W. B. Scott); Holbein (Yeames); Giorgio, painter in majolica, d. 1552 (Hart); Michael Angelo (Sykes); Primaticcio, the Italian who made the decorations at Fontainebleau, d. 1570 (O'Neil); Jean Goujon, to whom is attributed the old carving in the Louvre, d. 1572 (Bowler); Titian (Watts); Palissy (Townroe); François du Quesnoy, Flemish ivory carver, d. 1546 (Ward); Inigo Jones (Morgan); Grinling Gibbons (Watson); Wren (Crowe); Hogarth (Crowe); Sir J. Reynolds (Phillips); Mulready (Barwell).

SOUTH COURT, SHOWING THE PRINCE CONSORT'S GALLERY.

The only very modern artist in this list is Mulready, and he is certainly unfortunate, looking as if Mr.

Punch's most cynical artist had been employed to depict him. The late Mr. Owen Jones has been well represented in a mosaic set in the wall near a staircase leading from the Oriental Court decorated by him. Mulready is the only bit of really ugly work in the series, although, of course, the merits of the others are unequal. The artists have evidently given careful archæological study to the costumes of each period, and in some cases—as Prinsep's Giorgione, Scott's Vischer, and Pickersgill's Mantegna—the work is such as the grand old workers around need not be ashamed of. Of great interest, too, are the varieties of material of which the mosaics are composed, concerning which I can only say here that the Italian glass appears to me incomparably superior to the experiments in English ceramic wares.

The shape of this double room, it will be borne in mind, implies four large lunettes, one, that is, at each end of the two large roof-spans. One of these has been already filled by Sir Frederick Leighton, P.R.A., with an admirable allegorical painting representing the "Arts of War." Here we see workmen forging every variety of armor, shields, weapons, and women buckling them on to knights, as is written in fabliaux of the Round Table. Sir Frederick has put his most graceful drawing and purest colors into this fine work. There is also in the gallery a design for a companion picture of the "Arts of Peace," wherein the ladies are engaged in the pleasanter work of adorning themselves, and utilizing mirrors, while the men are toiling to provide the sinews for the gentler siege in which their own hearts are liable to capture. These works are scholarly, almost hypercritically exact in archæological details, and when the second is completed the court will be greatly improved.

To Mr. F. W. Moody, one of the most energetic and accomplished teachers at the museum, the institution is indebted for many instructive experiments and designs in the way of decoration. No one should fail to observe the very remarkable exterior wall decoration covering one entire side of the new School of Science, which is a most complete revival of the *sgraffito* work of the fifteenth century. This experiment by Mr. Moody of the

CHINESE POTTERS AT WORK.—WINDOW IN THE CERAMIC GALLERY.

high Renaissance in Italy has been placed on a wall of the building not visible from the streets, but only from the windows of the museum. It is analogous to the *niello*, which was graven in silver and the lines filled in with carbon, making a black picture on a white ground. (There is a good account of this ornamentation, said to be the origin of all engraving for printed work, in W. B. Scott's *Half-hour Lectures*.) Mr. Moody's experiment is made by filling in the hollows of the cement, presenting a multiplicity of scrolls, symbols, allegorical figures—Natura, Scientia, etc.—and portraits of scientific men. The stairway from which this vast work—covering the wall for four or five stories—can best be seen is another interesting experiment of Mr. Moody's. As befits a stairway leading to the Ceramic Gallery, its ornaments are made of Minton porcelain. The steps and facings of the steps are a kind of mosaic made of hexagon pellets painted; the walls are panelled with white porcelain; and their effect under the light falling through large figured windows, toned rather than colored, is very good indeed.

Entering now the Ceramic Gallery, we find its contents illustrated by a very ingeniously devised series of window etchings (as they may be called), which are probably unique in the history of work on glass. The windows on one side of this room, fifteen in number, each double, were intrusted to Mr. William B. Scott, who as an archæologist in art has few superiors. Mr. Scott designed no fewer than forty-eight large pictures, representing the history of ceramic art from the most ancient Chinese, Egyptian, Indian, and Persian down to Wedgwood; and these he has placed in the fifteen windows, where, unhappily, they are little observed, being without mention, much less description, in any work except that now before the reader. They are for the most part in black and white, colors being introduced only once or twice, and then but slightly. The first and second windows are devoted to the Chinese, their work being, if not the earliest, the most ancient in porcelain, and that which has most influenced the European art. Here is shown their whole method, from the preparation of the clay, the half-naked natives bringing the kaolm from caves in panniers, others steeping it in water, refining it in large mortars, and kneading it on tables. The potter is seen before his rude wheel, and forming the vessel by hand-pressure. And after this we trace his work to the furnace, and on to its place in the shop. This work implies the most patient study of original Chinese models. One window represents characteristic Chinese ornamentation—such as the royal dragon and the bird of paradise, and a bazar at Pekin. The third window represents early Egyptian art. The upper part shows the casting of brick by packing in boxes, and then turning it out, all under the whip of the taskmaster, the work and the whip being but little different to-day from what they were in the ancient days whose relics have been so diligently studied by Mr. Scott on the papyri of the British Museum. Beneath, a skilled workman is painting a large Canopus: he is on his knees, with his feet doubled behind him. One page, so to speak, of this window represents Assyrian art by a triumphal procession, in which immense vases are carried on ox trucks, and smaller ones on the heads of prisoners—a design based upon discoveries in Nineveh which show the great importance that people ascribed to earthenware. The fourth window is Greek and Etruscan. The Greek legend of the origin of painting—the daughter of the potter of Sicyon tracing on the wall the shadow of her lover on his leaving her for a journey—is exquisitely done. Next we see the girl applying her plan to her father's vases. We have also depicted with learning the honorary uses of pottery among the Greeks, the vases given as prizes in public games, or as votive offerings for the dead, by which custom the finest examples we have were transmitted; and, finally, there is the genius of Death holding in her hand the cinerary urn. The fifth window is Hispano-Moresque. The earliest ware in Europe after the Samian of which we have any examples was that made by the Moors, who brought the art of making it from east of the Mediterranean. This was the famous "lustre-ware" which was supplied from Spain, which is now so eagerly sought by collectors, both on account of its beauty and as the origin of the Italian majolica.

Specimens of this kind of pottery have been found by Layard at Nineveh and at Ephesus. There appears to be little doubt that it is of Persian origin. It must have been always very difficult to make; in the modern manufacture about fifty per cent. of the pieces come out of the furnace dull and worthless. The fine specimens seem to the workmen happy accidents rather than the steady results of any normal process upon which they can de-

ITALIAN MAJOLICA (URBINO). SIXTEENTH CENTURY.

pend. The first design in this window of Mr. Scott's represents the master-potter amidst his swarthy workmen watching the hour-glass beside the fire. This wonderful lustre was the result of some utilization of smoke in modifying the copper glaze, and was probably discovered by accident, as so many fine effects in the ceramic art have been. This beautiful ware has lately attracted especial attention in England because of the experiments which Mr. De Morgan, son of the late mathematician of University College, is making. He has tried nearly every kind of smoke influence upon copper and silver pigments, in contact with glaze and his success has been remarkable. These lustre-wares are still, I believe, made in some parts of Spain in a small way; also at Gubbio, in Italy; but the furnace of Mr. De Morgan at Chelsea is the most active and successful in bringing out such wares in all their varieties.

It adds greatly to the charm of these windows that they are as a frame around the objects whose history they tell. Fine examples of the "lustre-ware" from the earliest ages are in this gallery. And we have only to turn round from admiring another part of this fifth window, showing the building of the Alhambra, and its wonderful vase, to see the finest copy of that unparalleled piece of lustre-ware. The vase is four feet five and a half inches high, by eight feet two and a half inches in circumference; it is decorated with two antelopes, and foliations covering the body of the vase, intermingled with which are African characters whose sense is "Felicity and Fortune," "Permanent Prosperity;" and the colors are brown and blue on a yellow ground, the lustre being of a mother-of-pearl tint. From rich specimens of ancient Italian majolica we in turn refer to the sixth window, which shows us the embryonic and later phases of this beautiful art. The Italians imitated the Hispano-Moresque lustre as well as they could, but not being able to attain it exactly, they secured new tints of their own, especially a very fine ruby lustre. Afterward they painted their wares without trying to get lustres, to obtain which was perhaps a work too slow and precarious to be profitable. The vast development of ceramic art in Italy has required three windows—sixth, seventh, and eighth—for its representation. First we have bird's-eye views of the localities with which it was chiefly associated: Urbino, the seat of the finest ware made in the time of Raphael, wherein is portrayed their process of softening and refining the clay by putting it in square pits in the ground; Duranto, with its method of grinding the clay in a sort of water-mill; Gubbio, with its own ingenious processes. Then we have other Italian methods—foot-mill, hand-mill, horse-mill. An artist is seen in his studio, receiving as sitters ladies whose portraits he paints on plates that are to be their marriage gifts—a design taken from a plate in the gallery painted by Maestro Giorgio—while other details have been taken from a MS. by Piccolpasso, also preserved in the museum. And, finally, we have a representation of Luca della Robbia, of the fifteenth century, who used earthenware medallions, admirably modelled and fired with white glaze, which were fixed on the outside of buildings, and may be seen to-day on the Foundling Hospital and several churches at Florence. The very word "majolica" (Majorca) shows that the Italians found their art where the Moors left it. But if they could not equal the moresque lustres, they certainly developed and enriched their designs. Such decorations as that encircling the figure of St. George on the Urbino plate (see engraving) may be called "arabesque," but they are equally Italian. It is curious to compare such arabesques with the ornament on a piece of real Arabian work, such as the accompanying ancient lamp. (This lamp, singularly enough, is of a form represented in very early Italian bronze carvings of sacred subjects.) Window ninth is devoted to Dutch tiles and pots and Flanders-ware, which were once imported in such vast quantities to this country: here they may be traced from their manufacture in Holland to their sale in the Thames docks. Window tenth relates the curious story of the Dresden-ware. Here it was that the famous material of the best porcelain (kaolin), which was so long

LAMP FROM AN ARABIAN MOSQUE—
FOURTEENTH CENTURY.

the secret of China, was discovered by a happy accident—Böttcher, the alchemist, having taken a notion to analyze the white dust which his barber had used to powder his wig in a year of

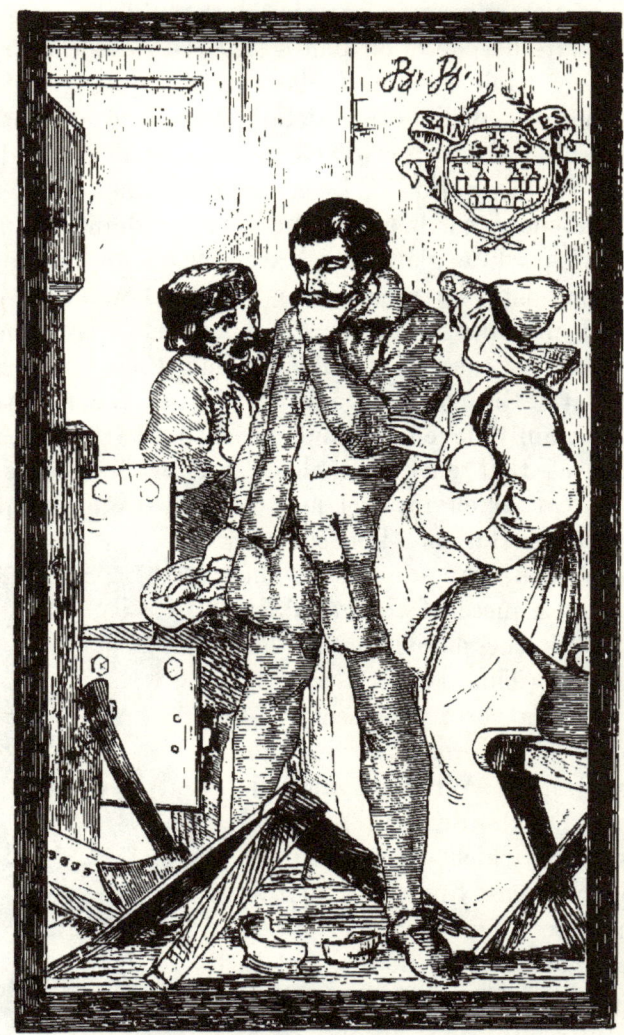

PALISSY, THE POTTER—WINDOW IN THE CERAMIC GALLERY.

dear flour. The two men are represented, and also the château of Meissen, where the first Dresden porcelain was secretly made. Window eleventh tells the story of Palissy, who, instructing himself, ruined his family: one leaf of the window shows him feeding his furnace with his broken furniture, while his wife with her babe stands beseechingly by; the other shows his triumph, as he builds and decorates the grottoes in the Tuilleries garden. The story recalls that of Benvenuto Cellini, who, having been seized with a fever while casting his Perseus and Medusa, heard that his work was ruined. Leaping from his bed, he found the furnace burst, but he saw the metal was partly fused; he cast in two hundred pieces of his table-service, and the mould was filled. The great work was saved, and so was the artist; he ate a hearty meal with his workman, slept soundly, and was himself again. Window twelfth is devoted to Sèvres, where porcelain was carried to its highest perfection. The famous "Rose du Barry" and "Bleu du Roi" are represented—and here exquisite colors are used—by Louis XV. and Madame Du Barry exchanging vases of those colors. The old manufactory is pictured, and some of its finest designs, in the lower panes of the window. Near by is the beautiful specimen of Sèvres which France contributed to the first International Exhibition in London. In window thirteenth we are introduced to English wares, at present the most excellent in the world. The processes described are —preparing the clay, making different colored clays, stamping tiles, filling color into moulds, "throwing," "turning," applying printed patterns. It takes two of the double windows to display this, which brings us to the fifteenth and last, in which there are four designs of the greatest historical interest: Dr. Doddridge's mother teaching her child Bible history from the tiles in the fireplace; Dr. Samuel Johnson trying experiments; figures of Josiah Wedgwood and Bentley, his partner; Flaxman and Stothard, the painter. The two artists

SÈVRES PORCELAIN VASE.—MODERN.

last named both worked in decorating earthenware for Wedgwood. Flaxman was underpaid by Wedgwood for the numerous models he supplied—models still used by the firm. The poor artist has made the fortunes of three generations of his employer's family, whose present representatives are so liberal that one must suppose their ancestor to have hardly realized the value of the artist's work until it was too late to reward him.

The visitor to the Ceramic Gallery in this museum will be apt to admit that there were never windows that shed more light than these of the kind required by a student. He will see lustres on the lustre-wares beyond what mere sunlight can give, and the huge dragons, deer, and horned birds on the Moresque-Spanish dishes will link the culture of 1882 with the barbaric mediæval mythology. He will, indeed, find at every step that he is really exploring in this gallery of pots and dishes strata marked all over with the vestiges of human and ethnical development. Nothing can be more complete than the arrangement of the gallery. Not only

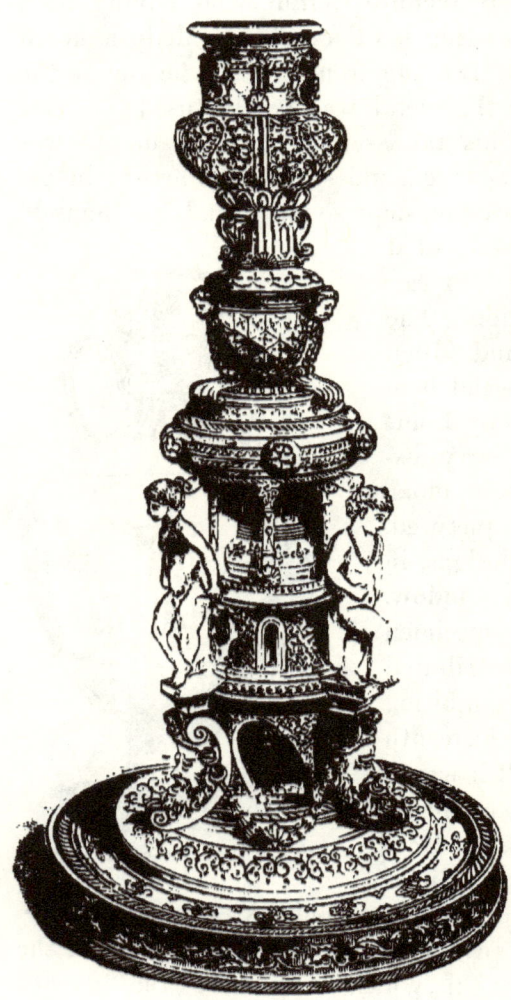

HENRI DEUX CANDLESTICK.

is it chronological, but beneath each particular specimen a card tells when and where it was made, and the price paid for it by the museum. If it has gone off with the floating collection, the card reports that also. One may learn what changes have occurred in the prices of such wares by finding Sèvres vases, for instance, marked at £100 or £200, of a like character with those six for which Lord Dudley recently paid £17,500. These are articles which, when first collected, incited the first cabinet minister who inspected them to ask, "What's the use of all this trash?" There is a single candlestick in this room now worth all the "trash" in that noble lord's mansion. It is a specimen of that famous "Henri Deux ware" of which only fifty-five pieces exist, so far as is known. This elegant ware has been such a puzzle to antiquarians that no fewer than thirteen different works have been written about it. It was finally ascertained by M. Riocreux, of the Imperial Ceramic Museum at Sèvres, that the pottery was made at Oiron, in France; that two artists made it in the earlier part of the sixteenth century for Henry II. and his queen, whose initials or monograms are on several of the pieces; and the artists were François Cherpentier and Jean Bernard. Cherpentier, the chief maker, had been an architect, and when he set about working in earthen-ware he was fond of moulding it in little monumental shapes, and filling in the hollows with different colors. The candlestick has a pale yellow ground, with arabesques, etc., in reddish-brown. The base is circular, with projecting brackets, on which stand three boys holding shields inscribed with the arms and cipher of Henri Deux. Above are three terminal figures of satyrs. This work (which it is to be hoped will some day be called by the artist's name instead of the king's) is less than a foot high; it cost £750, and is one of the cheapest purchases ever made. Seven of the fifty-five specimens of this ware are in the collection of Sir Anthony de Rothschild, two in that of Baron Lionel de Rothschild, two in that of Baron Gustave de Rothschild, three in that of Baron Alphonse de Rothschild, while the Louvre has the same number as the South Kensington Museum—five. Three very beautiful specimens (candlestick, ewer, and large salt-cellar) were found some years ago, very carefully wrapped in a blanket, placed in a wicker clothes-basket, under a bed in a garret of Narford Hall. Our engraving (p. 56) represents the candlestick so found. The pieces were no doubt collected by Sir Andrew Fountaine in France, in the last century, and, put away perhaps by some provident house-keeper, now turn up as a more valuable bequest to the old connoisseur's descendants than he could have imagined, but which is rightly appreciated by the present owner of the pieces, Mr. Andrew Fountaine. The other specimens of this Henri Deux ware in this gallery are two tazzas, a plateau, and a wonderful salt-cellar, of which last the skill of a pupil at South Kensington enables me to give the linear design.

HENRI DEUX SALT-CELLAR.

But it must not be supposed that this is merely an antiquarian collection: the best work now going on all over the world is represented, and one may see by the superb examples of modern Berlin work and of Minton that England and Germany are engaged in a competition for excellence which bids fair to distance anything done in the past. What admirable work Minton can do may be estimated by the embossed and tinted tiles surrounding the ten columns which support the roof of this gallery. They reproduce the finest colors of the Celadon porcelain of Sèvres. Around each column are letters forming the names of the ten greatest potters—Vitalis (whose name was found on a red vase of Samian-ware discovered in London in 1845), Giorgio Andreoli, Luca della Robbia, Veit Hirschvogel of Nuremberg (1441–1525), Xanto of Urbino (1547), Palissy (1510–89), François Cherpentier (maker of the Henri Deux ware, otherwise called faïence d'Oiron), Böttcher (1681–1719), Wedgwood (1730–95), and last, not least, Pousa, with whom began the list of wondrous accidents with which the history and traditions of pottery abound. Pousa is said to have been a workman in the imperial porcelain factory of China. On one occasion the emperor had ordered some great work, and Pousa tried long to produce it—in vain. Finally, driven to despair, he plunged into the furnace. His self-immolation caused such an effect upon the ware in the furnace that it came out the most beautiful piece of porcelain ever known. Pousa is now the patron saint of porcelain-workers in China, and is kept near them in a little corpulent figure (porcelain), which is familiar to many parts of the world where its story and sanctity are unknown. The South Kensington Museum has carried out in its own case this tradition of happy accidents, having been remarkable for its good-luck. Some instances of it are in the Ceramic Gallery. Some years ago a terrible explosion of gas occurred in the house of the famous art collector and dealer, Mr. Gambart, at St. John's Wood, by which the housemaid was killed. M. Alma Tadema was a guest in the house, and he had the presence of mind to open a window when he first perceived that gas was escaping, by which means the disaster was mainly limited to the dining-room. In this room were two large cabinets filled with splendid specimens of Flemish "graybeards," beakers, and similar wares, and some of the best were smashed. As the fragments were about to be cleared away, a friend of Mr. Gambart's, who was also connected with this museum, brought him an offer from the institution of £800 (as I have heard; at any rate, a sum that was generous) for the collection, broken and unbroken, and it was gratefully accepted. The skilled workmen at the museum have put the bits together with such adroitness that it requires a practised eye to distinguish the wares that suffered. The magnificent reproduction of the Alhambra Vase by Baron Davillier, elsewhere described, was exhibited at the Paris Exposition of 1867, and an agent of the museum found it "going a-begging;" he purchased it for far less than its actual value. And, indeed, I might instance a vast number of similar cases not only in this particular gallery—which we must now leave—but throughout the museum. The truth is, the South Kensington Museum has shown that the present is the great opportunity of museums, while it has done much to turn that tide on whose flood it floated to fortune, by awakening nations to the value of their treasures. The Oriental world, and, indeed, some portions of Southern Europe, have hitherto been unconscious of the value of their monuments, because only culture can prevent familiarity breeding contempt. Miss Frances Power Cobbe once expressed in my hearing the shock she received when, on first arriving at Old Alexandria, in Egypt, she found her luggage set down on an ancient monument resembling those treasured in the British Museum. How much the South Kensington Museum has reaped from the indifference to objects whose value is not intrinsic, and which for that reason are unique and inestimable, may appear incidentally as I proceed to describe some of them, adding what particulars I have been able to learn concerning their acquisition.

The little sixpenny guide-book sold at the door is necessarily provisional; the historical and descriptive volume which such an institution requires must remain a desideratum so long as the museum itself is changing and growing daily before our eyes. But the materials for that work exist; specialists have studied well the various departments; there exist nearly twenty large Blue-books recording the origin and growth of the museum; and when all these are sifted and their connected story told—enriched, as we may hope it will be, from the memories of those men who have founded and conducted the work to its present condition—the history so told will be in itself a sort of literary museum, replete with curiosities, picturesque incidents, and romance. In this scattered condition of the facts I have had to depend mainly on information given by the gentlemen just referred to, and what scraps I could pick up in old newspaper files and Blue-books. This it has appeared to me right to mention here, in explanation of any slightness and unsatisfactoriness that may be found in the details, or of the motley way in which they are put together.

If the history of this museum of civilization would record strange instances of popular neglect for great works of art, it must at the same time show that works of genius, in whatever perishable material embodied, have a strange vitality. The Milonian Venus, twice buried in the earth that she might not be harmed by the wrath of her Mars, has had experiences hardly more significant than those through which the sacred forms designed by Raphael—preserved by aid alike of king and regicide, by aid, too, of the neglect which left them hidden for a hundred years in lumber-rooms—have become the glorious inheritance of South Kensington.

The seven cartoons—what would not now be paid for the three that are lost!*—were designed and drawn by the great artist and his scholars at the request of Pope Leo X. (1513) as copies for tapestry, and the tapestries made from them are now in the Vatican. They were made at Arras, and the cartoons—so called because drawn on card-board—were thrown into the warehouse there. Here they remained neglected until they were seen by Rubens, who advised Charles I. to purchase them for a tapestry establishment at Mortlake, near London. On the death of the king, Oliver Cromwell paid £300 for them, intending that the tapestry-works should be continued. On the fall of Cromwell they were confiscated, and, for a second time, were thrust away into a lumber-room, this time at Whitehall. Fortunately the designs were on strips of paper twelve feet long, which could roll up, and so they were able to survive such usage. The next time they attracted notice was in the reign of William III., by whose order Sir Christopher Wren prepared a room for them at Hampton Court. They were then carefully lined with cloth.

---

* The "Stoning of Stephen," the "Conversion of St. Paul," and "Paul in the Dungeon at Philippi."

They were never removed again until placed in the gallery prepared for them here, with the sometimes criticised and certainly remarkable inscription beneath each, " Lent by the Queen." The last individual who clearly owned them was Oliver Cromwell, who paid what was supposed a large sum (£300) for works which no amount could purchase from the Protector's true heir —the English Nation.

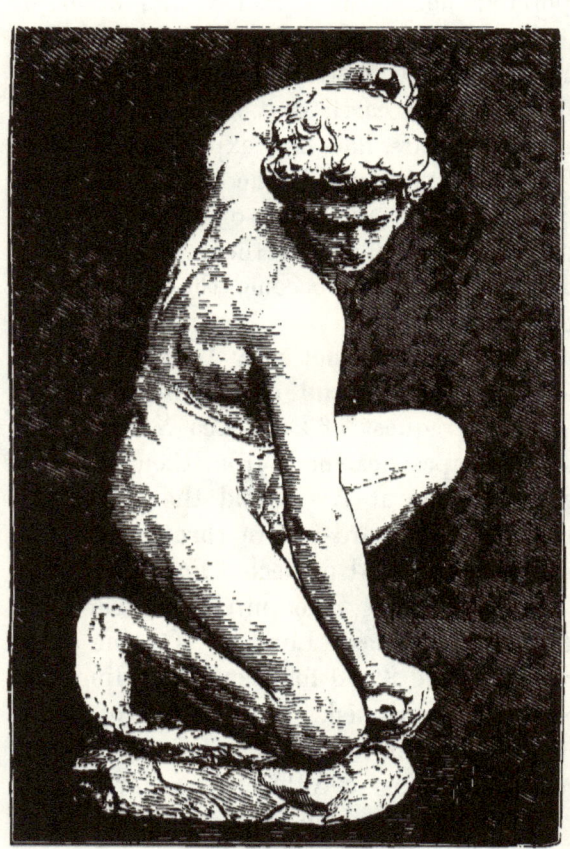

MICHAEL ANGELO'S EROS.

The museum is especially rich in old Italian glass. Some of these wine-glasses are nearly as light in weight as ordinary letter-paper, and the iridescence is most wonderful. One of the oldest forms has on it red Indian girls, dressed like Italian ballet-dancers of a very early period. There is reason to believe that this piece of glass was made soon after the discovery of America, when the enthusiasm about the region which the great Genoese had discovered filled all Italy. It is very plain that no portraits of the squaws could have reached the countrymen of Columbus when these dancers were designed. Mr. G. W. Cooke, Academician and landscape-painter, had in early life a studio in

Venice, and he had a way of picking up bits of old glass in the shops, the keepers of which were often willing, for a few soldi, to part with things now worth (in some cases literally) their weight in gold. Afterward he had, I believe, a studio in Agerola, and there also found beautiful Italian glass. He collected in this way enough to fill three or four large cases. After they were collected a considerable quantity of ancient Spanish glass was obtained, and the fact was made apparent that the latter was in some cases an imitation of the former—the reverse being probably the case with the majolica, in which Italy would seem to have imitated the Hispano-Moresque "lustre-wares." It is possible that a transfer of art-initiative from Spain to Italy may have been one of the first bad results of the banishment of the Moors, whose exquisite works are now models for our finest architects. With reference to the hypothesis that the theatrical squaws are to be referred to the interest that followed the discovery of America, I may mention that there are several curious instances in the museum where dates have been approximately fixed by the treatment of subjects. One notable example is a Japanese dish, on which is a rude but reverent representation of the baptism of Christ. Although certainty cannot be reached yet in the matter, it is possible that this dish was made before the extermination of Christianity from Japan (1641). However, it is known that before the discovery of kaolin in Europe the English and Dutch used to send over to China designs to be put on wares that were ordered. There are various pieces of china which are marked with English coats of arms, and a clergyman in Somersetshire has three pieces marked with scenes of the Passion. But I believe there is no instance where any such work is known to be Japanese, and, indeed, the latter had not formerly any great reputation in England.

There are eight magnificent Japanese bronzes in the museum, of which one is a figure of the beatified Buddha. It is impossible to gaze upon this grand figure (about fifteen feet high), seated with crossed legs, and open hands lying one in the other, without being impressed by a certain majesty in the ideal it represents, as well as astonished at the largeness of the undertaking which has produced a bronze of such size. The figure is seated, as it were, on the ground, and the round, infantine fulness and health of the face and the closed eyes render it probable that it was meant to represent the supreme moment when Sakya Muni attained, through humility and meditation, that sacred Buddhahood (enlightenment) which he had vainly sought by practising the severe asceticisms which the Brahmins enjoined upon him. "He met a certain Brahmin," says the Siamese version, "named Sotiya, and from him accepted eight handfuls of long grass. The Master spread the grass on the ground to the east of the Bo-tree, and sat thereon, and the grass became a jewelled throne. The Lord, with well-steadied mind, turned his whole thought to attain through purity and love the exaltation of knowledge. And around him gathered the angels of many worlds with fragrant offerings, and the strains of their celestial concert resounded in the most distant universe."

It is interesting to observe the strong impression made upon the casual visitors by this face so sweetly serene, so free from the lines which care and ambition trace upon the European face. I heard a little girl of thirteen years say, after her silent gaze, "How I would like to climb up and sit in his lap! Perhaps I would get some of his goodness." How many little ones of the East have felt the same as they looked upon this face of perfect holiness!

The history of some of the other bronzes is as follows: An English sea-captain saw three large bells, each seven or eight feet high, about to be taken on a Japanese ship for ballast. He saw that they were of antique and curious design, and was told that they had belonged to a temple that had been destroyed. The Japanese seamen gladly parted with them for a small sum, and told him of similar things near by. These, which were two bronze vessels something like huge candlesticks, each four and a half feet high—probably meant to support large masts for flags —he found lying amidst rubbish of old metal. These noble bronzes are elegantly modelled with dragon ornaments, and indicate a development of skill in this direction which has never been equalled in Europe. Besides these there are two large incense-burners eight feet high, and wonderfully wrought with beautiful decorative and symbolical forms.

But the indifference of the Japanese to their ancient relics is paralleled by that which prevailed in the cathedral at Bois-le-Duc, Holland, a few years ago, and led to the transfer to this museum of one of the finest specimens of the French Renaissance that now exist. In the rage for repairs the authorities of the cathedral pulled down this, its magnificent rood-loft—which is

MARBLE CANTORIA. BY BACCIO D'AGNOLO.

marked 1623, and consists of the finest colored marbles and many perfectly sculptured statues—and substituted for it a conventional Gothic structure. This great rood-loft—it covers one whole wall, sixty feet in width, and is from thirty to forty feet high—was actually carted out in pieces as rubbish, and lay in a corner of the cathedral yard, when some English tourist, attracted by the beauty of one of the statues, made a small offer for it, and finally purchased the entire structure for a few pounds. Finding some difficulty in carrying it off, the tourist wrote to the directors of the museum about it, and was overjoyed when they agreed to

TABERNACLE. ANDREA FERRUCCI.

purchase it for a thousand pounds. The museum was no less happy in securing for a tithe of its value this unique and admirable work, which is without damage of any kind, and stands in the New Court just as it did in the cathedral which was unable to appreciate its finest treasure. When the Queen of Holland recently visited the Museum, she was not a little disgusted when she came to this roodloft and heard its history.

Most of the "finds" by which the collection of ecclesiastical architecture has been enriched have been made in Italy. One of the most valuable of these is a Florentine "Cantoria," which has been affixed to the wall over the lower door-

ALTAR-PIECE.—THE VIRGIN WITH THE INFANT SAVIOUR.—ENAMELLED TERRA-COTTA, OR DELLA ROBBIA, IN HIGH RELIEF.—BY ANDREA DELLA ROBBIA.

way of the North Court, and thus supplying promenaders in the corridor above with a little balcony from which the contents of the great room below may be best seen. This singing-gallery was the work of Baccio d'Agnolo, and was set up in the Church of Santa Maria Novella, in Florence, about the year 1500.

In the neighborhood of the same city, namely, at Fiesole, the Church of San Girolamo was found willing, for small sums, to despoil itself of two fine examples of its own great artist (1490), Andrea di Fiesole, otherwise Ferrucci, and two works of the artist, not without honor save in his own country—an altar-piece and a tabernacle—grace an arcade of this museum. But the most precious possessions of this character are the specimens of Della Robbia ware, of which this museum has more than fifty examples. There were two men who gave this ware its name—Luca and Andrea, uncle and nephew—and their work is almost equally excellent. One of the pieces is a large terra-cotta medallion, eleven feet in diameter, bearing the arms and emblems of King René of Anjou, which was fixed in an exterior wall near Florence about fifty years before America was discovered, and, after undergoing the weather of over four centuries, its colors are as brilliant and its finest mouldings as clear as if it had been made this year. An altar-piece, probably by Andrea della Robbia, representing the Adoration of the Magi, is certainly one of the finest works of art, pictorially as well as in modelling, that have come to us from the era in which he lived. There are some twenty figures in relief, and each face has its own physiognomical distinctiveness, each head its phrenological peculiarities, all as carefully portrayed as if Lavater and Spurzheim had watched over the work. A figure of the Virgin and Child, with an arched border of fruit and flowers, presents us with an expression which could only be conveyed fully if the matchless colors could be transferred to my page, but which entitles it to be classed among those great Madonnas of art history which have influenced civilization.

The most conspicuous object in the North Court is the reproduction by Mr. Franchi of a pulpit erected in the cathedral at

Pisa by Giovanni Pisano in 1302–11. A fire occurred in the cathedral in 1596 by which this great work was damaged, and the panels—carvings in relief of Scripture subjects—were deposited in the crypt; other parts of the pulpit were removed to the arcades of the Campo Santo, and some others incorporated in the new pulpit of the cathedral. Some ten years ago Mr. Franchi, of whose wonderful skill the museum contains many evidences, obtained from the cathedral authorities permission to take casts of all these scattered parts of Pisano's greatest work, and having done so, he put them together; and now, more than two centuries and a half after the structure vanished from Pisa, it has been set up at South Kensington. The reproduction has been so perfect—even to the toning of the marble (as it seems to be) by age—that no one could imagine it to be a reproduction. And it was certainly worthy of all this care. The supports of the circular tribune are groups of statues—Fortitude, holding a lion by the tail, head downward; Prudence, with compass and cornucopia; Justice, with scales; Charity, nursing twins; Temperantia, who, oddly enough, is quite nude and in the Medicean attitude; and the Evangelists. The statues, two-thirds the size of life, are grouped around eight columns, which they nearly conceal. At the top of these the tribune is enclosed by seven large panels, in which are finely carved the Nativity, the Adoration of the Wise Men, the Presentation in the Temple, the Massacre of the Innocents, the Betrayal, the Crucifixion, the Resurrection. This noble work justifies the ancient fame of Pisa as the home of sculpture.

HERCULES, THE DUKE OF FERRARA.

The museum is particularly rich in Michael Angelos, considering that it has had to glean after the Glyptothek of Munich, the Vatican, and the Louvre. It possesses the beautiful Eros (see page 62) executed in the great sculptor's twenty-fourth year (1497), also his statuette of St. Sebastian, unfinished, and showing the last touches of his chisel—as, without the intervening appliances of modern sculpture, he carved his idea directly on the marble. There is a female bust ascribed to him, and another work in which he participated, which is quite unique: this is a case of small models in wax and terra-cotta, of which twelve are by Michael Angelo. This case was for a long time in the Gherardini family, and was purchased by a Parliamentary grant in 1854 for the sum of £2110. One of these little models is that of the slave. Buonarotti's two slaves or prisoners, the originals of which are in the Louvre, are here in good copies, the one exhibiting the physical suffering of the fettered man, the other the mental anguish of bondage. There are also admirable casts of other works by the same artist, the finest being the colossal figure of David, which stands in the new Tribune at Florence. This copy was presented to the museum by the late Grand Duke of Tuscany, and is one of the many excellent fruits which have been gathered from the international league which European princes have entered into for the purpose of exchanging works of this character, and reciprocally aiding in the work of enriching the museums which constitute so important a feature of modern civilization. It is a happy characteristic of this museum that one meets in it very few objects whose interest or beauty is marred by association with war. The spoils are few, the tokens of friendship with foreign nations innumerable. Some pieces of work in gold brought back from Abyssinia and from the kingdom of Ashantee—the latter close to the famous umbrella of King Koffee—were exhibited, and a few of them remain here to show by their exquisite chasing that blows aimed at so-called savages are likely to fall upon the springing germs of civilization. The poorly designed but wonderfully chased and jewelled symbols of Theodore excited general admiration. The bird that was perched on the top of King Koffee's state chair is also of fine workmanship. It is rude in design, truly; but it is hardly ruder than the gold dove, the ampulla which holds the oil used at English coronations; and perhaps, like the latter, it purposely imitated a primitive and consecrated form. These African trophies are unpleasantly suggestive of the worst phase of British policy, or impolicy; but they are slight incidents in a museum which

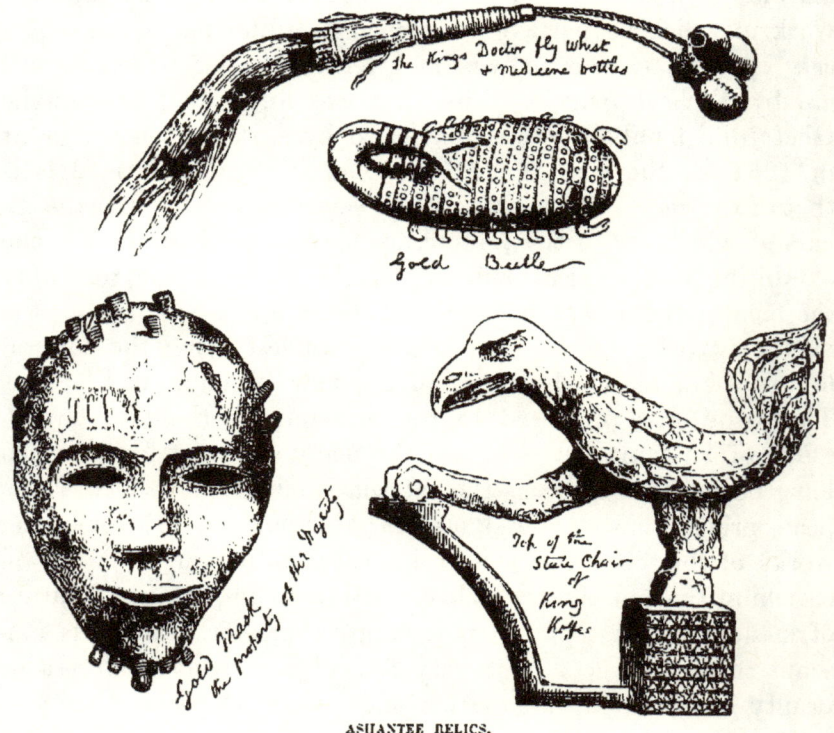

ASHANTEE RELICS.

will forever be considered the ripest fruit of the long Victorian and victorious era of Peace.

It is quite impossible for me to invite my reader to an exploration of the loan collections. Some of the ancient jewellery and gold work which has been, or is, shown here is not only intrinsically priceless and beautiful, but also historical, *e. g.*, the Mexican sun-opal; the largest known aqua-marine, set as a sword-hilt, formerly belonging to the King of Naples (Joachim Murat); a cat's-eye (largest known), formerly belonging to King Candy; a piece of amber in which is a small fish—all of which have been

THE CELLINI SARDONYX EWER, MOUNTED IN ENAMELLED GOLD, AND SET WITH GEMS—ITALIAN. SIXTEENTH CENTURY.

loaned by Beresford Hope, M.P. But the great treasure belonging to this gentleman, and long exhibited here, was the famous Cellini ewer. Previous to the great Revolution, it was part of the crown-jewels of France, and Mr. Hope has recently sold it to a collector in that country. This matchless work is ten and a half inches in height; the body is formed of two convex pieces of carved sardonyx, with a similar piece for pedestal; the handle and spout are of gold, covered with masks and figures richly enamelled, and set with rubies and diamonds. In place of this fragment of old French royalty, which the explosion sent flying and the Republic has lured back, is the brilliant gold missal case of Henrietta Maria. Some of the most beautiful specimens of ancient *repoussé* gold work and enamels were, until recently, in a case made up chiefly from the collection of Mr. Gladstone, whose fondness for things of this kind, though rather indiscriminate, has done something to popularize the taste for them. In a recent Christmas satire, "The Fijiad," the Prime Minister has been portrayed rather cleverly in his right environment:

> "Great Homer's bust upon the table stood —
> Homer much talked of, little understood;
> Around the bust were ranged, with curious care,
> Gems of old Dresden or of Chelsea ware,
> Cracked teapots, marvels of ceramic art,
> Choice Faïence and Palissy set apart;
> For great Gladisseus, warrior of renown,
> For plates and pottery ransacked the town,
> Made dowagers and virtuosi stare,
> Collectors, jealous, tear their scanty hair."

When the Gladstone collection was brought to the hammer, it did not require many hours for the same cases to be refilled with objects quite as beautiful from the large accumulation which the museum always has on hand or obtainable in excess of its present room for their exhibition. It is rather droll, however, to find one of Mr. Gladstone's specimens of sacred art replaced by a wonderful racing prize, a silver cup three feet high, representing the "Birth of the Horse." The winged steed is rampant on top, while the gods and goddesses of Olympus gather around it in homage. It is modern English work, and would do for an allegorical representation of the august divinities of Parliament adjourning to honor the American winged winner of the Derby in 1881.

One of the most important loan exhibitions ever opened at the museum was completed at the end of May, 1881. It consists of Spanish and Portuguese ornamental art. On my way to visit this exhibition I read in a daily paper the invitation extended by the present King of Spain to the Jews of Russia to take refuge from their persecutions in the Peninsula from which they were so cruelly expelled three hundred and eighty-nine years ago. The first object which met my eye in the exhibition was

CHÂSSE, OR RELIQUARY—LIMOGES ENAMEL. THIRTEENTH CENTURY.

traced with the spirit which led to that inhuman decree. It is a large altar-piece, or retable, painted in distemper on panel, in seventeen Gothic compartments, the subjects being from the legend of St. George. It is of wood, twenty-two feet in height, sixteen feet in width, and is from a destroyed church in Valencia. One of the three centre compartments represents James I. of Aragon rescued by St. George in battle against the Moors. At the bottom there are ten compartments painted with subjects from the life of Christ. In these pictures the figures and faces of the Jews have been carefully mutilated. Jesus and his disciples remain to prove how beautifully the artist had done his work; the hacked and scratched figures around them remain to attest that in the fifteenth century, to which the work belongs, fanaticism was strong enough in Spain to invade the altar and destroy the most beautiful works by which Art was seeking to soften human ferocity. In one of the panels Jesus, with a face of utmost benignity, is represented receiving the kiss of Judas on his left cheek, and at the same time extending his right hand to touch the ear of Malchus. This servant of Caiaphas would seem, from so much of him as is left, to be in a half-kneeling posture. Peter, with angry face, holds over Malchus his short sword. One may see here the spirit of fanaticism making its choice between the gentle healer of wounds and the fierce inflicter of them. Upon this stony hatred the Inquisition built its church. The knife which hewed and hacked the Jewish figures of these once beautiful panels was presently mutilating the Spanish Jews themselves. In 1492 the greatness and littleness of Spain culminated together: by the nobility of Isabella, Columbus was enabled to discover America; by the meanness of Ferdinand, the Jews and the Moors were driven out of Spain with every circumstance of inhumanity.

And now King Alfonso wants them back. There was once an Alfonso who thought he could have suggested a better world than this, if the Creator had consulted him; the present Alfonso will not be censured for thinking he could have created a better Spain than was fashioned by the Inquisitors. One need only look around upon this wonderful collection of Spanish objects of art to see that it was Spain's self as much as Jews or Moors that the sword of fanaticism mutilated and disfigured. Here is the splendid *débris* of arts which Moorish genius and Jewish wealth combined to render possible. From the time of their expulsion Spanish art suffered a progressive decline. Dark and symbolical seems the purple velvet banner of the "Holy Office" sent here by Madrid, where it used to be carried in procession to every *auto-da-fé*. On it embroidered angels hold the instruments of

Christ's suffering, which Inquisitors turned upon humanity, and the inscription is, "Clamans voce magna emissit spiritum." The color of this strange banner is that of blood grown darker with time. It came from the side of crucified humanity. But it was Spain that breathed out its spirit, now loudly recalled.

Of the Moresque porcelain I have already spoken in pages of this work written before the Loan Exhibition was opened. Suffice it to say that there are here the best specimens of that lustre-ware in existence. "During the sixteenth century," says Señor Riaño, "the Spaniards did nothing but imitate what was done in other countries."[*] In the seventeenth century, when a Spanish pictorial art was born with Velasquez, Murillo, and Zurbaran, it was reflected in some of the wood-carvings, notably in those of Alonso Cano. The most artistic piece of such work at South Kensington is a statue of St. Francis of Assisi by that artist; it is carved in walnut, and exquisitely painted. Lady Charlotte Schreiber has loaned a remarkable circular jewel, sixteenth century, of which there is a legend. When Charles V. was visiting the northern towns of his paternal duchy, a Frisian gentleman, Governor of Harlingen, named Humalda, warned him against embarking on the Zuyder Zee with some troops he was despatching to the opposite shore. The emperor reluctantly yielded; the tempest Humalda predicted arose, and every man was lost. Charles said to Humalda, "Thou art my Star of the Sea" (*sternsee*); and afterward had this jewel made for the Frisian, who thenceforth assumed the name Sternsee, borne by his descendants. The jewel represents Charles V. standing on a star-spangled orb, rocked by the Devil from below, and at the sides figures of Death and War. The inscription around it is, "Carolus V. Sternsee. In te Domine speravi."

Many of the inscriptions found upon Spanish ornamental works were in Cufic characters even after the banishment of the Moors. The workmen seemed to realize the value of letters

---

[*] "Catalogue of Spanish Works of Art in the South Kensington Museum in 1872." By Señor Juan F. Riaño, of the Educational Board of the Ministry of Fomento, Spain. Reprinted in Mr. Robinson's Catalogue of the Loan Exhibition of 1881.

which made beautiful fringes while they conveyed meanings. But it is only in ancient Hispano-Moresque carvings that the Cufic inscriptions are found in their perfection. An ivory casket, eleventh century, is covered with deeply-cut figures of conventional birds and animals, and around the margin of the lid is a Cufic inscription saying, " In the name of God. The blessing of God, happiness, prosperity, good fortune, perfect health and peace of mind, perpetual pleasures and delight to the owner of this casket." Another ivory box has round its dome-shaped cover, " I display the fairest of sights. Beauty has cast upon me a robe bright with gems. Behold in me a vessel for musk, for camphor, and ambergris."

On the opposite side of the hall, facing the altar-picture of the disfigured Jews, is a great reredos from the high altar of the cathedral of Ciudad Rodrigo. It was painted about twelve years before the discovery of America, it is believed, by Fernando Gallegos, greatest Spanish painter of that century, and three assistants. This picture also has traces of disfigurement which have their story to tell. It is owned by Mr. J. C. Robinson, to whose explorations of Spain and enthusiasm for antiquarian art this fine exhibition is mainly due. Mr. Robinson's account of this picture shows that its injuries came by English guns, in 1811, during the Peninsular War. The cathedral stands near the fortress of Ciudad Rodrigo, and the English shot traversed it from end to end. The grand reredos was so injured that a new one was erected. Twenty-nine of the panels, though in some cases perforated, were preserved separately in a corridor of the chapter-house. In 1879 they were sold to a local dealer, who forwarded them to Madrid, whence they were brought to this country. In some of the panels the faces and costumes are Moorish. It is still a magnificent work, and must originally have been over fifty feet high, by twenty-five in width. Its panels, beginning with Chaos and the Creation of Eve, pass at once to the life and Passion of Christ. It is likely that this monument of so many eras, thus curiously brought to the country which marred it, will not be followed by many similar treasures. The Spaniards have lately learned the value of such things. The Spanish collection made at South Kensington by Mr. Robinson, for a long time superintendent of the art-collections, chiefly led to the formation of the Archæological Museum at Madrid. When Mr. Robinson began his visits to Spain (about 1862) things were in a fair condition for foreign collectors. "At the period in question," he says, "railways had scarcely yet made their appearance in the Peninsula, photography was almost unknown, and the country was not overrun by the professional dealers, native and foreign, who have since ransacked every nook and corner of the land. On the other hand, in these comparatively early days of the collecting furore, facilities for the discovery and purchase of specimens were few, and the work of acquisition slow and difficult. A few brokers and silversmiths alone occupied themselves casually in the commerce of antiquities in Madrid, Lisbon, and one or two other of the chief cities. Neglect and destruction were still the rule. Ancient things, once out of use, if their materials had any intrinsic value, were forthwith demolished and utilized. The fine enamelled jewels of the sixteenth century were often broken up for the stones and the gold. The most admirable works in silver were currently consigned to the smelting-pot; the splendid iron 'rejas' were converted into mules' and asses' shoes; and the gorgeous carved and gilded wood-work of dismantled churches and convents burnt for the sake of the bullion to be derived from the rich gilding on its surface." This is now all changed, and the Peninsula boasts its band of dealers as well organized as any in Europe; nor is it behindhand in their shadows—the fabricators of fraudulent specimens of the kinds most in request.

The visitor to South Kensington should bear in mind that there may be Loan Exhibitions in some of the adjacent buildings of a highly important character. As I write there is a collection on exhibition which will well repay a visitor for the exploration required to reach it, for it has had to find rooms on the west side of the Gardens: this is the anthropological collection gathered by General Pitt Rivers, who, before he became heir of the late Lord Rivers, had made the name of Lane Fox so noble in the scientific world that one almost regrets that his good-fortune, in which all rejoice, involved a change of name. In this collection the evolution of savage and barbarian weapons, ornaments, utensils, and the like may be studied. General Pitt Rivers has arranged boomerangs in series, so that the completest form may be traced back to the first slightly curved stick found to carry some increase of force. The development of a shield from a mere stick grasped in the hand, next with a protection for the hand, may be traced. There is a series of paddles upon which may be followed a human form, degraded from one surface to another, until a grotesque conventional figure appears on the last without a trace of human semblance. The ornamental marks on the bodies of pots are found in some instances to have been suggested by the net-work print left by their corded holders. These are but a few instances of the way in which objects are made by a man of science to tell their own history. Among the articles which have received the attention of General Pitt Rivers are the caps worn by the women of Brittany, and a few supplementary cases of these have been added to his wonderful collection. An examination of these caps—which are considered of so much importance that a woman is not allowed to enter church without one, nor with one of a pattern belonging to another parish—shows good reason for the supposition that their sanctity is derived from their having been all developed from the head-dress of the nun. Such is the opinion that General Pitt Rivers expressed when he conducted me through his rooms. He showed me that each cap has parts which correspond to parts of the normal cap of the nun. These parts have grown small in some cases; in others they are pinned up; but in the latter case they are let down on important occasions—funerals and weddings—and the wearers are then all nun-like.

These little French things, however, are hardly to be included in this great collection—perhaps the most important private collection of objects illustrative of anthropology in the world. Nor is there any book more useful to the student of anthropology than the illustrated and explanatory catalogue of 1247 of these objects prepared by General Pitt Rivers, and published by the Science and Art Department.*

Various public men sent their treasures to the museum in its earlier days, when they were more needed than now; but it has been found necessary to select fastidiously from the too numerous articles offered every year as loans. Many families owning valuable collections find it difficult to keep them in perfect safety, and more begin to realize that such articles should not be of private advantage. Some collections, originally received as loans, it is pretty certain will never be removed; and I am assured by the director that the museum has been notified of being remembered in many wills. This gentleman, Sir Philip Cunliffe Owen, and his predecessor, Sir Henry Cole, said to me, in conversation about the prospect of building museums in the American cities, that they had no doubt such institutions, if good and safe buildings were erected, would there as well as here find themselves centres of gravitation for the art treasures and curiosities owned by the community around them. This museum, though hardly out of its teens, has received seven great collections, worth collectively more than two million dollars; thirteen bequests, worth over half a million dollars; and a large number of donations whose aggregate money value is very great, though not yet estimated. Among the more important donations six-

---

* Since this was written General Pitt Rivers has offered his grand collection to the nation as a free gift, and I am ashamed and astounded to learn that it has been declined! The great men connected with the South Kensington institutions—Huxley, Poynter, Cunliffe Owen, and others—were felicitating themselves at this splendid acquisition, when this mysterious refusal came. Sir John Lubbock, as I write, is questioning the Government on the subject, and it is possible the outrageous folly may be checked. I regret to say there are indications that the cause of it is a certain jealousy that has sprung up in influential quarters at the prodigious growth of the South Kensington collections. For the moment they have managed to make the British Museum a sort of dog-in-the-manger. I cannot believe, however, that the country will consent that such jealousy shall become a contest so costly to itself. The incident I have just mentioned tempts me to strike out from this work some complimentary things I have written concerning the administration of the Science and Art Department; but the facts have not yet been publicly sifted, and I leave what is written in hope that the result of this strange affair may not turn all its admiration to satire.

teen have been from the Queen, nineteen from the late Prince Consort, three from Napoleon III. (very valuable too—Raphael's "Holy Family," in Gobelin tapestry; four pieces of Beauvais tapestry, and a collection of 4854 engravings from the Louvre), three from the Emperor of Russia, and thirty Egyptian musical instruments from the Khedive. Thirty-one donations, including, of course, a much larger number of objects, have been received from twenty-eight governments. In this list Japan (two), Würtemberg (two), and the United States (three) are the only governments which appear more than once; but I am sorry to say the presents of the American Republic are limited to department reports, the last being one from the War Department on gunshot wounds. Twenty European museums have sent valuable gifts to this youngest member of their family. Among private individuals, other than the donors of collections, Sir Henry Cole, K.C.B., father of the museum, and

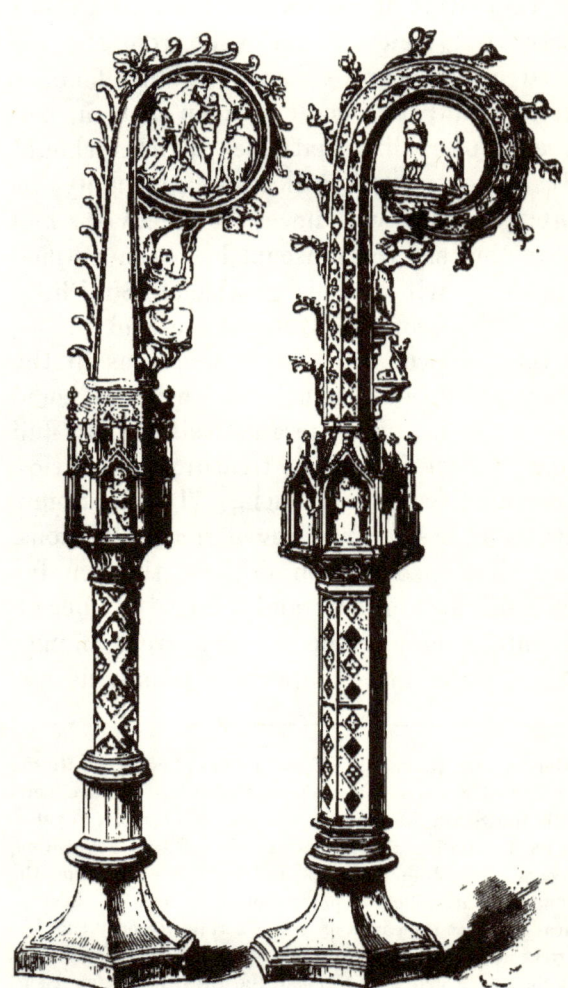

PASTORAL STAVES—IVORY AND ENAMEL. FOURTEENTH CENTURY.

his family, are represented by twenty-eight valuable gifts—gifts, however, which are little compared with the enthusiasm and intelligence they lavished on the institution they saw planted as a seed, and may now from their windows behold grown to its present large proportions.

Among the numerous gifts and bequests which the museum has received during the past twenty years the following are the most important:

In 1857. By John Sheepshanks, Esq., 233 oil paintings, 289 water-color paintings, etchings, and other drawings. (Gift.) Mr. Sheepshanks died in 1863.

In 1860 and in 1873. By Mrs. Elizabeth Ellison, 100 water-color drawings. (Acting in the spirit of the intention of her late husband, Richard Ellison, Esq., of Sudbrook House, Lincolnshire.) For the purpose of forming a National Collection of Water-color Drawings. (Gift.)

In 1864. By Rev. R. Brooke, 396 objects, consisting of textiles, watches, rings, etc., and 718 volumes of books. (Gift.)

In 1867. By Mrs. Wollaston, 270 drawings of mosaics. (Gift.)

In 1867. By W. Minshull Bigg, Esq., 3 works in marble by Lough: "Puck," "The Melancholy Jaques," "Titania." (Bequest.)

In 1867 and 1868. By Sir Charles Wentworth Dilke, Bart., M.P., 297 volumes, 862 pamphlets, and 155 prints illustrating the Great Exhibition, 1851. (Gift.) Died in 1869.

In 1868. By Mrs. Louisa Plumley, 43 enamel paintings by Essex, Bone, etc. (Bequest.)

In 1868. By Professor Ella, 329 volumes of music, printed and in MS.; 6 busts, 1 oil painting (a portrait of Rossini). From the Library of the Musical Union Institute. (Gift.)

In 1868. By Rev. Chauncy Hare Townshend, 211 objects, chiefly jewels, 189 oil paintings, 174 water-color paintings, 4218 Swiss coins, 831 volumes, 390 drawings, 1815 prints. (Bequest.)

In 1869. By Rev. Alexander Dyce, 80 pictures, 63 miniatures, 802 drawings, 1511 prints, 74 rings, 27 art objects, 13,596 books. (Bequest.)

In 1870. By William Gibbs, Esq., Roman and Anglo-Saxon ornaments and other antiquities, chiefly found in Kent. (Bequest.)

In 1870. By Alfred Davis, Esq., a collection of coral. (Bequest.)

In 1870. By John Meeson Parsons, Esq., a collection of 92 oil and 47 water-color paintings. (Bequest.)

In 1871. By C. T. Maud, Esq., 6 oil paintings of the English School. (Gift.)

In 1871. By W. S. Louch, Esq., 2 oil paintings, 2 water-colors, etc. (Bequest.)

In 1871. By W. Smith, Esq., 86 early English water-color drawings. (Gift.)

In 1872. By Thomas Millard, Esq., 197 gold and silver coins, chiefly English. (Bequest.)

In 1872. By Mr. Tatlock, 15 drawings and paintings by De Wint, and by Hilton. (Gift.)

In 1872. By Lady Walmsley, 13 oil paintings. (Gift.)

In 1873. By C. T. Maud, Esq., 11 water-color drawings. (Gift.)

In 1874. By Alexander Barker, Esq., Venetian furniture of a boudoir. (Bequest.)

In 1875. By Assimon, Delavigne, et Cie, a collection of French lace. (Gift.)

In 1875. By Mrs. A. Nadporojsky, a collection of Russian lace. (Gift.)

In 1876. By John Forster, Esq., 48 oil paintings, 74 frames of water-color paintings and drawings, collections of drawings, sketches, and engravings; collection of manuscripts and autographs, library of printed and illustrated books.

In 1876. By Sir M. Digby and Lady Wyatt, 148 fans. (Gift.)

In 1876. By William Smith, Esq., 136 water-color drawings, and also 700 volumes.

In 1882. By John Jones, Esq., pictures and virtu amounting to £240,000. (Bequest.)

For the purpose of industrial and art education, the museum has found the perfect casts and reproductions that can now be made not inferior in value to original works. In this respect the international convention, to which reference has already been made, has been of immense advantage. As one of the signs of better times, to be set against standing armies, the agreement deserves insertion in any account of this museum. It was entered into during the Paris Exposition of 1867, and in the following year communicated by the Prince of Wales to the Lord President of the Council:

CONVENTION FOR PROMOTING UNIVERSAL REPRODUCTIONS OF WORKS OF ART FOR THE BENEFIT OF MUSEUMS OF ALL COUNTRIES.

Throughout the world every country possesses fine historical monuments of art of its own, which can easily be reproduced by casts, electrotypes, photographs, and other processes, without the slightest damage to the originals.

(*a*). The knowledge of such monuments is necessary to the progress of art, and the reproductions of them would be of a high value to all museums for public instruction.

(*b*). The commencement of a system of reproducing works of art has been made by the South Kensington Museum, and illustrations of it are now exhibited in the British section of the Paris Exhibition, where may be seen specimens of French, Italian, Spanish, Portuguese, German, Swiss, Russian, Hindoo, Celtic, and English art.

(*c*). The following outline of operations is suggested:

I. Each country to form its own commission, according to its own views, for obtaining such reproductions as it may desire for its own museums.

II. The commissions of each country to correspond with one another, and send information of what reproductions each causes to be made, so that every country, if disposed, may take advantage of the labors of other countries at a moderate cost.

III. Each country to arrange for making exchanges for objects which it desires.

IV. In order to promote the formation of the proposed commissions in each country, and facilitate the making of reproductions, the undersigned members of the reigning families throughout Europe, meeting at the Paris Exhibition of 1867, have signified their approval of the plan, and their desire to promote the realization of it.

The following Princes have already signed this convention:

Great Britain and Ireland.. { Albert Edward, Prince of Wales.
{ Alfred, Duke of Edinburgh.

Prussia	Frederick William, Crown Prince of Prussia.
Hesse	Louis, Prince of Hesse.
Saxony	Albert, Prince Royal of Saxony.
France	Prince Napoleon (Jerome).
Belgium	Philippe, Comte de Flandre.
Russia	The Czarowitz.
"	Nicolas, Duc de Leuchtenberg.
Sweden and Norway	Oscar, Prince of Sweden and Norway.
Italy	Humbert, Prince Royal of Italy.
"	Amadeus, Duke of Aosta.
Austria	{ Charles Louis, Archduke of Austria. { Rainer, Archduke of Austria.
Denmark	Frederick, Crown Prince of Denmark.

PARIS, 1867.

Cincinnati is already sharing these reproductions; and the signers of the above document would gladly have the Governors of the American States which possess museums add to it their names, and transatlantic museums avail themselves of its advantages. These advantages are very great, as, after one cast has been made, the cost of the rest amounts to little more than that of material and transportation. This kind of work is now done in such perfection that it were easy for an untrained eye to doubt which is original and which reproduction. The firms officially connected with the Science and Art Department always use marks which have a money value in Europe. For three or four pounds any museum or private collector may obtain perfect copies of ancient shields, salt-cellars, tankards, tazzas, fire-

ELKINGTON'S MARK.   FRANCHI AND SON'S MARK.

dogs, knockers, whether chased or *repoussé*. Old specimens of this kind are rare and costly. A beautiful pair of bronze firedogs—pedestals surrounded by Cupids, and supporting respectively Venus and Adonis—made in Venice about 1570, are rather costly, the work being intricate and the figures four feet high; but Franchi's copper-bronze copies at £30 are nearly as good as the originals, which were considered cheap at the £300 paid by the museum. A wonderful old Italian bronze knocker (1560), fourteen and a half inches in height and thirteen inches wide, which cost £80, is reproduced by the same firm for £4.

It is, however, the large casts of Oriental objects and ancient German shrines that will probably be of paramount interest to an American. It is here shown that the most notable and interesting objects in the world can be copied with the utmost exactness, and in their actual size, and brought within reach of the people of any country. Even Trajan's Column is here; and, though in this case it has had to be set up in two columns instead of one, many others have confirmed my experience of the impossibility in tracing out at Rome the figures which cover it so satisfactorily as they can be made out at South Kensington.

The 17th of May, 1880, is an historic day in the annals of the museum. On that day was thrown open to the public its Indian section. A small collection of Indian curiosities has long been wandering from one place to another in London, and had finally been shelved at the very top of the India Office. So, at any rate, it was stated, and most persons were willing to accept the statement on faith by the time they reached the third story of that edifice. However, the collection steadily increased up there, and it was at length removed to some rooms at South Kensington. But there it attracted little attention from the public, though much from scholars, and it was publicly announced that it would be closed because it did not pay expenses. The authorities ultimately followed better counsels: they gave it up to the Direction of the South Kensington Museum. The Queen loaned it the magnificent collection of Oriental armor from Windsor Castle; Indian treasures hitherto dispersed through the other courts of the museum were gathered together in the new section; Dr. Leitner's collection of Græco-Buddhist sculptures was added; the walls adorned with Carpenter's water-colors illustrative of Indian scenery and life; and lo! London awaked one morning to find that it had a new and splendid institution, which the Queen and her family had visited the day before with "the greatest satisfaction."

It is indeed a noble section; and if any one has read about

India, is at all interested in its pantheon, its mythology, or its relation to the evolution of humanity, he may pass many fruitful days or even weeks in these wonderful rooms. There is no university in the world where one can learn so much about India, especially if he should study these objects in connection with Fergusson's *History of Indian and Eastern Architecture*. Immediately on entering, one passes those strange remains brought by Dr. Leitner from Peshawar, which exhibit the influence of Greek art upon India at the time when Buddhism was there in its zenith of power. Next we pass beneath the model of the great Sanchi Tope Gate. The Buddhist Tope is a sort of mound or barrow, only built of earth and stone with great care; it is shaped like a regular dome, surrounded by a double railing, and is reached through four large gates of the finest and most elaborate carvings. This hill-like dome, wherever found, appears to have no other use than to contain some tiny relic—one of Buddha's hairs, say, or his toe-nail. In the *Mahawanso*, the Buddhist history of Ceylon, it is said: "The chief of the Devos, Sumano, supplicated of the deity worthy of offerings for an offering. The Vanquisher, passing his hand over his head, bestowed on him a handful of his pure blue locks from the growing hair of his head. Receiving and depositing it in a superb golden casket, on the spot where the divine teacher had stood, he enshrined the lock in an emerald dagoba, and bowed down in worship." The thorax-bone of Buddha is a great relic; but most sacred of all is his left canine tooth, whose shrine probably originated the famous Car of Juggernaut. Among the treasures in this section is a drum-shaped reliquary of pure gold; it is about three inches high by two in diameter, and panelled with saints in relief. It was found in one of these huge topes; inside it were wrappings within wrappings, and last of all some hardly distinguishable speck representing an unknown saint.

The model of the great gate is probably the largest achievement of the copying art ever known. In 1869 the party set out with twenty-eight tons of materials, chiefly plaster-of-Paris; these were drawn by bullocks one hundred and eighty miles; and in a year's time three full-sized casts of the magnificent structure were completed without a flaw—which is marvellous, considering the extremely fine and complicated character of the carvings. This structure, erected in the first century of our era, is thirty-three feet in height. There are two high pillars—every inch of whose surfaces is covered with symbolical carvings—supporting capitals made of elephant-heads—the elephant being the animal in whose shape Buddha descended for his incarnation. Above the elephants three cross-beams are stretched, upholding pinnacles bearing the phallic Trisul, the Wheel, the Lion. There are winged lions that remind us of Assyrian influence; there are sieges and wars (no doubt about the relics); scenes relating to the princely and amorous years of Siddharta, but nothing of his asceticism or his lowliness; everywhere symbolical forms, especially the serpent, which is always intertwined with the emblems of early Buddhism, indicating that his first converts were the serpent-worshippers called Nagas. The intricacy and fineness of all this work, constituting, as Fergusson has said, the "picture Bible of Buddhism," are indescribable.

Throughout this Indian section there are large photographs of the temples and palaces representing the eras of Indian architecture—Buddhist, Dravidian, Jain, Moslem—and near many of them actual specimens or casts of their ornamentation. Some of these specimens of sculptured ornamentation fill one with amazement at the degree of art-culture they imply, and by their refined beauty. Here the capital of a pillar is fringed round with small elephant-heads; there a pedestal is adorned with mounted horsemen in relief, so regularly dispersed that at first they might hardly be noticed. There are some architraves from Rajpootna, of the eleventh century, made up of gods, goddesses, and symbolic forms, the tracery of which is so refined and the execution so delicate that it would be impossible to find any European work of like antiquity to equal it. These arts are still kept up. There are some screens from Mirzapore and from Agra, made of perforated sandstone or marble, which are meant for ventilation and also to admit a little light: they are so delicate, and the figures so fine-edged, as to induce one to touch them and make sure they are not made of paper or wax.

Dr. Birdwood has prepared in two small volumes a fair handbook of this section, which, however, contains no direct references to the objects. Useful as it is, a student will find that it is too apt to take the conventional view of things, as, for example, when it speaks of Hindoos throwing themselves beneath the Car of Juggernaut — an error which Dr. Hunter exploded long ago. There is no doubt that the real way to understand these objects, and to derive high benefit from this unique collection, is to study them in connection with Dr. Fergusson's great work on Eastern architecture — certainly one of the greatest archæological and descriptive books ever written.

The throne of Akbar was set in the air at the convergence of bridges, so that no man might approach him without being inspected from the surrounding windows, and any arms he might have about him observed. Before removal to the new section it stood in all its grandeur, but it has been considered sufficient to preserve the central column and the large capital which supported the famous throne. It is wonderful, indeed, that it should be left to this age and to England to appreciate the romance of the East, and to revise, correct, and estimate the traditions of the Oriental world concerning its own monarchs. Akbar, for instance, bears the reputation in the East of having been an archtyrant and a blasphemer, and the care he took in preparing this curious building, with his throne suspended, as it were, in mid-air for safety, is regarded as confirming the Oriental view. But the fact is now known that the hostility excited by Akbar was through his liberality in entering upon a comparative study of all religions, arousing thereby the enmity of all their priesthoods. From being a saint, to whom the people brought their sick that his breath might heal them, the Emperor became in popular regard a demon. He instituted at Delhi (A.D. 1542–1605) discussions on every Thursday evening, to which he invited the most learned representatives of all religions, allowing each his statement with strict impartiality; he had as many as he could of the sacred books of each religion translated for his library, though neither his threats nor bribes could extort from the Brahmans their Vedas, which now are open to every English reader through the labors of Max Müller. He tried in turns worshipping Vishnu, Allah, the Sun, and Christ. Badáoní writes that "when the strong embankment of our clear [Mussulman] law and our excellent faith had once been broken through, his Majesty grew colder and colder." This sad result (in the view of Badáoní) being proved by the fact that "not a trace of Mussulman feeling was left in his heart," and "there grew gradually, as the outline on a stone, the conviction in his heart that there were sensible men of all religions."

He had three wives representing these religions — Mehal (Hindoo), Roumi (Moslem), Miriam (Christian). A great deal of Akbar's toleration and independence may be ascribed to the influence of his favorite sultana, Mehal. She was a faithful, wise, and educated lady, who always held the Emperor to his high standard. There is a miniature of her in this museum, showing her in a rich gauze, or dress, diaphanous above the waist; she is not burdened with jewels, as was the case with some of her wealthy subjects, but wears the ornaments of a lowly and quiet spirit.

There is also here a picture of the superb tomb, the Taje, at Agra. It is the most beautiful monument in the world; even that of the Prince Consort, in Hyde Park, is poor beside it. It is to be remembered, however, that, according to the imperial custom of that period and region, such tombs were built while those for whom they were intended were yet living. They were by no means what Western people would imagine to be tombs, but beautiful pleasure-domes of purest marbles. During the lives of their builders they were wont to invite their friends to gay feasts in them, and this continued until the pretty palace received the dead bodies of those who had enjoyed them, and were so turned into monuments.

It is not always that these ancient monuments, as in Akbar's case, survive to remind the world of to-day what forerunners some of its characteristic tendencies had in early times and unsuspected places. Indeed, it might surprise some of the magnificent princes of the East in the far past if they could now visit London and observe the kind of interest their monuments excite. Here, for example, is an exact and full-sized copy of that ancient iron pillar of Delhi which some think gave the province its name. It was set up in the fourth century, and is twenty-two feet above ground. All manner of superstitions have grown around it. The Hindoos have a belief that it rests upon the head of the king-serpent Vásaki, near the earth's centre; that the founder of a great dynasty was told by an oracle that if he planted it there his kingdom would never be shaken so long as it should stand; that one of his successors, doubting this legend, dug it up, and found the bottom stained with the serpent's blood; and that in consequence the dynasty passed away before Mussulman and then English conquerors. For ages this pillar has been kept polished by the vast numbers who climbed or tried to climb it every year, success in this feat being deemed a proof of high pedigree. But during fifteen centuries there were two rather obvious things which the Hindoos appear never to have attempted—one was to really dig about the bottom of this pillar, the other to translate an old Sanscrit inscription on it. Both of these have recently been done by Englishmen. The bottom was found to reach only twenty inches beneath the surface of the earth, there resting on a gridiron of iron bars. The inscription testifies that it was set up by a prince unknown in other Hindoo annals. This prince, Dháva by name, would appear to have been the most extraordinary being that the sun ever shone upon, or, rather, that ever shone upon the sun. A clause of the inscription runs: "By him who obtained with his own arm an undivided sovereignty on the earth for a long period, who united in himself the qualities of the sun and the moon, who had beauty of countenance like the full moon—by this same Rajah Dháva, having bowed his head to the feet of Vishnu, and fixed his mind on him, was this very lofty arm of the adored Vishnu [the pillar] caused to be erected." There was probably a figure of Garuda on it originally, which the Mohammedans would have removed; but the real object of the pillar, Mr. Fergusson thinks, was to celebrate the defeat of the Balhikas (A.D. 364 or 371). "It is," says Fergusson, "to say the least of it, a curious coincidence that, eight centuries afterward, men from that same Bactrian country should have erected a Jaya Stambha ten times as tall as this one, in the same court-yard, to celebrate their victory over the descendants of those Hindoos who so long before had expelled their ancestors from the country." The chief present value of the monument of this magnificent individual is the light it enables such archæologists of metals as Day, Percy, Murray, and Mallet to cast on the early use of iron. It is pure malleable iron, without alloy; and though since it was forged it has been exposed to the weather, it is unrusted, and the capital and inscription are as clear as when it was set up fourteen centuries ago. Mr. Day has shown the remarkable interest of this pillar in that respect, though I believe that the iron sickle found beneath the feet of a Sphinx, and now in the British Museum, brings us nearer to Tubal-cain by a thousand years, being assigned to B.C. 600.

The Indian section has sundry "trophies," among which the "Tippoo Tiger" is conspicuous. As it is just possible that some transatlantic readers may be so benighted as not to know what the "Tippoo Tiger" is, I will explain that it is a musical instrument contrived for the delectation of Tippoo Sahib. It is a large-sized tiger, under whose claws lies a prostrate Englishman, dressed pretty much in the fashion of a London City merchant of East India Company times. When this emblematic organ is played the music that issues consists of blended tiger-growls and human groans. This instrument was made for Tippoo Sultan by a fellow-citizen of the tiger's victim! It brought much satisfaction to the royal breast of Tippoo, and still more perhaps to the boys who used to be taken to see and hear it when it was a show in Leadenhall Street. Not far from it is also a beautiful cannon which belonged to Tippoo Sahib; it was captured at Mysore, and presented to the Queen. Instead of the cross with which the godly guns of Christendom are decorated, this one is adorned with the sun and moon; but it has also a lion, to remind Britannia where her own emblem may have originated. Tippoo Sahib's throne was supported by massive gold tiger-heads, admirably wrought, one of which is also in the Windsor collection. He would seem to have been fond of animals.

There is in the Oriental fire-arms a notable resemblance to the old arquebus. It looks as if when the Orientals received gunpowder from the West they received also the cross-bows with which it was first connected; and, while that shape has been completely modified here, it has been retained in the East. The powder-horns and other accoutrements also have a curious resemblance to the mediæval shape of such things in Europe.

Prominence is given to another "trophy," the throne of Runjeet Singh, whom the English overthrew. It is a large throne, wrought of pure gold, and too softly cushioned to have ever fulfilled the much-needed duties of that Eastern throne whose velvet seat turned to rough flint whenever any subject of him who sat on it was suffering an injustice.

There are a good many things in this Indian section which one meets with surprise. For example, here is a tablet of marble which belonged to the Parsees of Bombay, but is decorated with Assyrian figures; also, there is a panel brought from the Audience Hall of the Great Mogul, on which is fashioned in marbles of various colors a fair copy of Orpheus charming the beasts with his violin, as it was found frescoed in the Catacombs. It is surmised that Austin de Bordeaux, who worked for a time at Delhi, copied it from Raphael's picture, and made Orpheus a portrait of himself. But it is not so easy to explain the close resemblance between the ancient pottery of Gour and the Della Robbia ware.

The collection of jade in this section is superb; it cannot be worth much less than fifty thousand pounds. The splendid jewellery, the rich stuffs, the models of Hindoos of all castes, the conventionalized figures of the deities, the pottery of all times and places in India here collected, make this new section one of unique interest, and one which cannot fail to prove of importance to the industrial arts as well as to Oriental studies.

South Kensington Museum contains a noble collection of Persian articles, ancient and modern, made for it in that country by Major R. Murdoch Smith, of the Royal Engineers. I say ancient and modern: but where an art has had a continuous evolution it would be perhaps more philosophical to pronounce its last results the oldest, and its "modern" period that in which it was newest.

MODERN PERSIAN EWER (COPPER-COATED, WITH WHITE METAL).

In no other part of this museum have I seen works which reminded me so much of that long conspiracy between man and nature by which wild-briers have turned to roses. It seemed to me there might be written on the walls this beautiful page of the "Rose Garden" of Sâdi: "I have heard that in the land of the East they are forty years in making a china cup: they make a hundred a day at Bagdad, and consequently you see the meanness of the price. A chicken, as soon as it comes out of the egg, seeks its food; but an infant hath not reason and discrimination. That which was something all at once never arrives at much perfection; and the other by degrees surpasses all things in power and excellence. Glass is everywhere, and therefore of no value; the ruby is obtained with difficulty, and on that account is precious. Affairs are accomplished through patience: the hasty man faileth in his undertakings."

It was probably under the inspiration of these very words of Sâdi that Bagdad in the end vindicated itself. "The powerful Abbaside Caliphs of Bagdad," says Major Murdoch Smith, " no doubt summoned to their court men of science and learning from all the countries under their sway—Persia furnishing them with architects and other artists. Skilled Persian workmen were no doubt employed in large numbers in decorating the mosques and palaces in the Arab capital, situated as it was on the very frontier of their own country. Thence, we believe, arose the so-called Arabian or arabesque style of ornament, afterward so widely spread, and now so well known. The peculiar pendent ornamentation of vaults and niches, of which the Alhambra is so typical an example, is identical in style with that used throughout Persia down to the present day." If this theory be true—and really these works appear to sanction it—the Arabs derived their arts from Persia, as the Romans did from the Greeks, and consequently the Moors imported a Persian art into Spain. The Shah of Persia, in wishing to carry back with him Owen Jones's reproductions of the Alhambra at the Crystal Palace, had good reason for his selection.

OLD PERSIAN EARTHENWARE (WATER-BOTTLE).

It is difficult to tell the age of most of this Persian work, and I think the enterprising collector of these specimens is not always happy in his estimates. Thus there is a beautiful vase (No. 1224) which Major Smith thinks over 500 years old, on the ground that it bears an inscription in Pehlevi; but that is no more evidence than would be a Latin epitaph in Westminster Abbey that the monument was erected during the Roman occupation of Britain. The collection shows that Persian art is by no means in such a state of decay as many have supposed. This is especially true of the exquisite damascene work still executed at Ispahan. "The true damascene," says our collector, "is made of a particular kind of iron. After the object is forged it is placed for six or eight days in the furnace of a hot bath, where the greatest attention has to be paid to the even heating of the article. The bath is heated with the dried dung of cows and other animals, which gives a steady and not very intense heat, and is supposed to contain the salts necessary for the formation of true damascene. When the article is taken out of the furnace it is left at the temper it has therein acquired. It is then finished and polished. To bring out the grain a certain mineral (of which a specimen may be seen in the museum) is then applied in the following manner: about three parts of the mineral are dissolved in ten of water, over a slow fire, in an earthenware or leaden vessel. The object is then slightly heated, and a little of the liquid applied with a cotton wad, after which it is washed in cold water. If the damascene does not appear sufficiently the operation is repeated. The object must be thoroughly cleaned and polished before the mineral is applied."

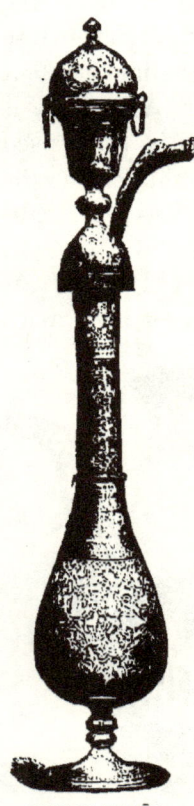

PERSIAN KALIÄN.

It is very doubtful if Corsinet, the French artist who carried the art of damascening to such an extent in the time of Henry IV., has left any such beautiful work as this now being wrought by artists whose names are unknown in Europe. The three kinds of ornamentation known as "damascening" are elegantly represented — the delicately lustred and watered blade, the light etching on polished steel, and the rich inlaying of steel with gold and silver. One of the most beautiful pieces of work is a kaliän or hookah (for smoking tobacco) of brass open-work, with turquoise and other ornamentation. In the head of this great and solemn pipe the tobacco is placed, slightly moistened, under pieces of live charcoal, which are prevented from falling off by the movable top of the bottle containing the water, into which the end of the stem descends. The tobacco smoked is the mild Tombaku, produced near Shiraz, which really is the best "Turkish," though Turkey never produced a leaf of it. If any one will gaze on this Persian hookah he will see why it is imposing enough to warrant such religious treatment as its Indian counterpart, the hubble-bubble, has received at the hands of an eloquent Vedantist preacher of my acquaintance (Chintamon). The hubble-bubble is generally made of a cocoa-nut shell, with a receptacle for water, through which the smoke passes before being inhaled. In Chintamon's parable the stem represents the body; passions are the tobacco; the bowl is mind; understanding is the plug which prevents the tobacco-passions from blocking up the stem-body; knowledge is the fire which separates passion—the pure from the impure; the evil is reduced to ashes, and vanishes in the vapor of folly; while through the purifying water of reflection, and the mouth-piece of mental satisfaction, man draws the desirable aroma of content, and hears a bubbling noise which suggests the still small voice of Reason.

ANCIENT PERSIAN INCENSE-BURNER (PIERCED AND CHASED BRASS).

Among the many exquisite books, manuscripts, and paintings—the latter being oftenest upon the covers of the finest books—there is one of surpassing beauty. It is a copy of the works of Sádi, a modern manuscript with six illuminated pages forming the head-pieces of the six books, all the pages being bordered in gold and colors. The covers have been painted by the artist Nadjaf, who lived about fifty years ago, on the outside with certain battles between some shahs, sultans, and their like; but on the inside of one cover is a picture of the poet Hafiz surrounded by his friends; on the inside of the other cover is a picture of Sàdi conversing with his pupils. What grace, what honor, was in the heart of him who drew these pictures! Amidst such tints Sàdi might be saying to his pupils one of the passages that are here written: "I saw a peacock's feather in the leaves of the Koran. I said, 'I consider this an honor much greater than your quality deserves.' He replied, 'Be silent; for whosoever has beauty, wherever he puts his foot doth not every one receive him with respect?' A little beauty is preferable to great wealth."

MODERN PERSIAN INCENSE-BURNER (BRASS).

I hear of some prosaic young Englishmen who are wandering about the banks of the Euphrates to try and find the locality of Eden. I venture to affirm that with the Kaliān, plenty of Tombaku, Sàdi's Gulistan, and this rose-garden manuscript, I can get nearer Eden reclining on yon English grass than those young gentlemen seeking it so far away. Yet it is pleasant, in a melancholy way, to see the never-failing fascination which the Oriental world has for these Northern races. The hardest, least imaginative Englishman will feel some sweeter pulsation about his heart when he sees one of Holman Hunt's pictures of Palestine, or hears the solemn roll of Oriental poetry.

> "A pine-tree's standing lonely
>   In the North, on a mountain's brow,
> Nodding with whitest cover,
>   Wrapped up by the ice and snow.
>
> "He's dreaming of a palm-tree,
>   Which, far in the Morning Land,
> Lonely and silent sorrows
>   'Mid burning rocks and sand."*

But here my rambles through these unlimited fields must draw to a close. One must, amidst such numberless treasures gathered from the great streams of Time, more especially remember Sydney Smith's advice, based on the post-diluvial brevity of human life, that writers should "think of Noah, and be brief." It is with a certain distress that I feel compelled to pass by the great galleries of pictures, including some of the finest Turners, Wilkies, and Gainsboroughs, and a large number of historic paintings. The Forster bequest, with its charming souvenirs of famous actors, actresses, and authors, in the shape of portraits, character-sketches, and autographs —among the latter the MSS. of most of the works of Dickens—were of itself the sufficient theme for a treatise.

ANDREA GRITTI, DOGE OF VENICE—ITALIAN. ASCRIBED TO VITTORE CAMELO. SIXTEENTH CENTURY.

No collection in the museum is more deserving of attention than that of the musical instruments, which show the entire evo-

---

* Heine. Translated by Charles Leland.

TAZZA—ALGERIAN ONYX AND ENAMEL. MODERN FRENCH.

lution of the art, from the first savage bark drum and the pipe that Pan might have played to his flocks, up to the last grand piano; but for twelve shillings the reader may procure Mr. Carl Engel's admirable *résumé* of this department. Since it was written an interesting series of instruments has been added (Indian section), and it is to be hoped that these will be included in a new edition of Herr Engel's work. The Indian instruments have not changed in many centuries, some not for two thousand years; their harp (chang) is identical with one represented in the Nineveh sculptures. Unfortunately there is no catalogue to the museum; but there may be had full works on the ancient ivories (one guinea), textile fabrics (one and a half guineas), majolica (two guineas), furniture and woodwork (one guinea). There are small shilling "Handbooks," giving succinct histories of the arts of working in gold and silver, bronze, pottery, etc., with general reference to objects in the museum, which are useful and interesting. There also exists a full catalogue of books on art (two guineas); and I may mention that at the present moment it is possible to collect in London an admirable art library for a moderate sum—an advantage that will soon disappear. The present art library in the museum is the only one possessing anything like

SALT-CELLAR—SILVER GILT; ITALIAN. FIFTEENTH CENTURY.

completeness in Europe; it contains 45,000 volumes. This is quite distinct from the educational library, which has an equal number of volumes.

But we must not part from South Kensington without considering how fares therein the aim and purpose out of which it grew, namely, culture and training in every variety of art. It will at once be recognized that the art schools, enjoying such an unparalleled environment as to examples, carried on also in rooms of vast extent, perfectly lighted, heated, ventilated, and furnished, must be judged by a higher standard than other institutions of the kind in Europe or in America. And, retrospectively, the schools must be conceded to have done wonders. For one thing, it may be claimed that it found the art education of the nation at zero and raised it enormously. By wisely using its power to send floating through the provincial cities a loan exhibition, and by a judicious distribution of the annual fund (now about £2500) granted it by Parliament to aid institutions of a like character, which are willing also to aid themselves, the Commission has been the means of establishing throughout the kingdom schools devoted to art, and in forming classes in colleges to teach art, to an extent which has increased by 150 per cent. the number of those who study art to prosecute it for itself, or to apply it to make their work more artistic. Between the years 1855–'77, 27,000 objects of art and 24,000 paintings were circulated by the museum through the United Kingdom. In the various provincial towns and cities where they have been left for several months at a time, these works have been visited by over 6,000,000 of per-

IVORY TANKARD—AUGSBURG. SEVENTEENTH CENTURY.

sons and copied by many students, the cost to the Science and Art Department being over £100,000. In order to tempt Schools of Art to acquire permanent objects for museums of their own, the Department offers a grant in aid of fifty per cent. on the cost of such objects. Parliament is continually inquiring into the means of increasing the utility of the collections in this direction. South Kensington has already awakened a higher taste throughout the nation, and especially in London. The number of visitors has increasingly exceeded a million each year; and should the museum be opened on Sunday afternoons—a step which can hardly fail to be taken ere long—this number must be vastly increased. These crowds, however, never make the rooms seem crowded; their decorum is equal to that which is preserved in the best drawing-rooms; there have been only two cases in the history of the museum where persons have been ejected (the fault being tipsiness); and no article of value has ever been missed. In strolling through the building with George Boughton we concluded to follow some very rough-looking youths and observe what objects attracted their attention. We were surprised to find them passing by King Koffee's umbrella and trinkets to devote all their time to the statues of Michael Angelo. I have repeatedly observed similar phenomena in the picture-galleries—the roughest people crowding around the best works of art.

The way in which all this has told upon the work of the country has been jealously watched, and also fairly recognized by foreign critics. The first gold medal awarded on the Continent for art education, awarded to South Kensington, was not given by any favor, and it was won by a great deal of hard work. In the introduction to the seven-volume report presented to the French Government in 1862, M. Chevallier says: "Rivals are springing up, and the pre-eminence of France may receive a shock if we do not take care. The upward movement is visible, above all, among the English. The whole world has been struck with the progress they have made since the last Exhibition in designs for stuffs, in the distribution of colors, also in carving and sculpture, and generally in articles of furniture." M. Rupet urged the establishment of a museum in Paris similar to that at South Kensington, saying: "It is impossible to ignore the fact that a serious struggle awaits France from this quarter." The report from Lyons—whose School of Design was, to a large extent, the model copied by England—says: "With Great Britain we shall have some day to settle accounts, for she has made great progress in art since the Exhibition of 1851." These statements are much more true now than when they were written. In the direction to which they refer—that of decorative art—South Kensington has certainly taken a leading position in Europe. The evidences of this are appearing daily. For example, the firm of Messrs. Corbière & Sons, which was established in London about twenty-eight years ago as an importing house for French patterns and goods, has now been almost changed into an exporting house, sending to France patterns and designs for goods which it obtains from South Kensington. Even this is hardly so grateful to the English as a report lately made by a large Glasgow firm, that it has for some years been obtaining from this museum, at the annual cost of a few hundred pounds, designs such as it had been for many years previously securing from Paris and Lyons at a cost of £2000 per annum.

Lyons, indeed, after teaching England its art of war, has itself lost it. Neither Paris or London will use their newest patterns, one of which, I understand, represents huntsmen and hounds in full chase after a stag, careering all over a drawing-room carpet! In Paris, and even more in England, taste has for some years been tending to demand richness in substance, vagueness in pattern, quietness in color, for all stuffs used in rooms. It is greatly to be regretted that the great manufacturers of textile fabrics declined to participate in the Centennial Exhibition, having concluded that their goods would have too much protection in one sense, and not enough in others. It would have excited astonishment in America to see what transformation has been wrought in carpets and curtains, and it would be at once recognized that the old fabrics, with their fixed scrolls, their glare and glitter, have become barbarous. Messrs. Ward, of Halifax, recently rolled out for me on a floor side by side the old patterns and the new, and it was to the eye like passing from poppies to passionflowers. "Those blazing ones," said Mr. Ward, "have gone out of fashion in this country since the new schools of design began, and we never sell a yard of them here; we made them

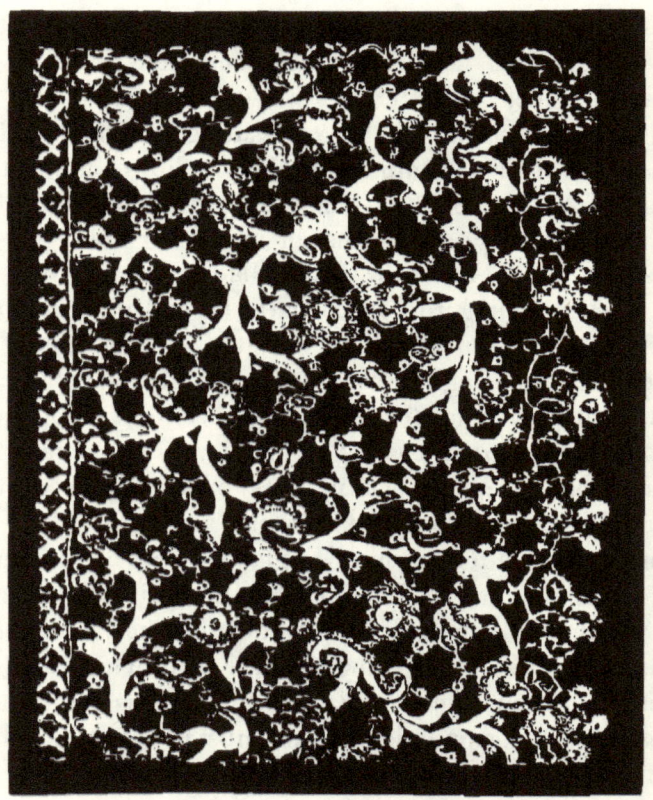

FINEST RAISED VENETIAN POINT LACE—FLORAL DESIGN. ITALIAN. SEVENTEENTH CENTURY.

for America until the last tariff, and now the manufacture has ceased altogether." The new curtain stuffs have always an unobtrusive, almost a dead, ground of saffron, or olive, or green, and on it flowing conventional leaves with some heraldic form —as daisy, pomegranate, etc.—to supply spots of color; and the carpets are of much the same character, with somewhat larger forms.

These exquisite designs are universally recognized as results of South Kensington. But there is one point where the results are less satisfactory. The best designs, which include the human figure, have still to be obtained from the Continent; and these being of especial importance in pottery, the great porcelain factories say that their needs cannot yet be met by English art schools. The truth is, there was long an opposition in controlling quarters to permitting studies of the female nude at South Kensington at all, though now the female students have that privilege. In the male school the male nude is studied; but still the students—those who mean to devote themselves to fine, as distinguished from decorative, art—have to unite and employ female models in rooms outside the school. It is as difficult to see what benefit is secured by modesty, in thus placing a necessary study beyond the regulation of the masters, who might preserve decorum, as it is to find any advantage to religion gained by shutting the door to the pictorial gospels of Raphael on Sunday and keeping open the door of the gin-shop. Both the piety and the prudery are anomalous. The Zoological and the Botanical Gardens, in London, the Dublin Museum, Hampton Court, and Kew Gardens are all open on Sunday, while the museums and galleries of the metropolis are closed: the Royal Academy has nude models of both sexes, under the same Government which prohibits the like at South Kensington. The queerest anomaly, however, existed until lately in the Slade School of Art, at University College, where the vexed question was settled by permitting the male pupils to have female models, and the female pupils to have male models! This restriction of the ladies to (nearly) nude models of the other sex was made in the interest of propriety, as the masters felt disinclined to enter and instruct them in the presence of a female model.

The former restrictions at South Kensington as to models fell heavily upon the female pupils. The young female artists were not permitted to see so much of their model as they would be required to reveal of their own persons at one of her Majesty's drawing-rooms. The late head-master, Mr. Burchett, himself an able figure painter, knew well, as all experienced figure painters in Europe know, that female models are far oftener secured from vice by their occupation than exposed to it, and that life schools are not inconsistent with decorum, under proper management; and he (Mr. Burchett) made efforts, one of which was to have the model encased in flesh tights, to secure for his pupils the advantages so freely offered in Continental schools. But his contrivances were stopped by threats of Parliamentary questions. His successor has, however, secured to the female pupils the advantage of the nude model of their own sex and male model with *caleçon;* and, if he can now secure like privileges for the males, South Kensington may some day be able to point to as high results in the direction of the fine as in the ornamental arts. Until then young men of genius will continue to prefer schools which are without such restrictions. It can only be ascribed to the consummate care with which studies of the antique are conducted, and to the full supply of the finest casts offered by the museum, that decorative art itself at South Kensington has suffered so little from the limitations referred to; for it is certain that the human figure is the key to all other forms in nature. It is certain, also, that the female form is the very flower of all natural beauty—"the sum of every creature's best," as Shakspeare says of Perdita—and no arrangements for art training can be considered complete which do not include accessibility to such studies of the same as are required, by those who have given evidence of their fitness to interpret the sacred secrets of nature.

Beyond this there is no special deduction to be made from the method of training at South Kensington, which as a school is steadily improving. The following official memorandum of its regulations (with which is given the names of its faculty) will show the large scope of instruction included:

DIRECTOR-GENERAL FOR ART, AND PRINCIPAL,
THOMAS ARMSTRONG.

Head-Master, J. SPARKES.
Mechanical and Architectural Drawing, H. B. HAGREEN.
Geometry and Perspective, E. S. BURCHETT.
Painting, Free-hand Drawing of Ornament, etc., the Figure and Anatomy, and Ornamental Design, J. SPARKES, C. P. SLOCOMBE, T. CLACK, F. M. MILLER.
Modelling, M. LANTERI.
Etching, A. LEGROS.

FEMALE CLASSES.

Lady Superintendent, MISS TRULOCK.
Female Teachers, MRS. S. E. CASABIANCA and MISS CHANNON.
Occasional Lecturers: DR. ZERFFI, Historic Ornament; E. BELLAMY, Anatomy; F. W. MOODY, the Figure, as applied to Decoration.

1. The courses of instruction pursued in the School have for their object the systematic training of teachers, male and female, in the practice of Art and in the knowledge of its scientific principles, with the view of qualifying them to impart to others a careful Art education, and to develop its application to the common uses of life, and to the requirements of Trade and Manufactures. Special courses are arranged in order to qualify School-masters of Elementary and other Schools to teach Elementary Drawing as a part of general education concurrently with writing.

2. The instruction comprehends the following subjects: Free-hand, Architectural, and Mechanical Drawing; Practical Geometry and Perspective; Painting in Oil, Tempera, and Water-colors; Modelling, Moulding, and Casting. The Classes for Drawing, Painting, and Modelling include Architectural and other Ornament, Flowers, Objects of still-life, etc., the Figure from the Antique and the Life, and the study of Anatomy as applicable to Art.

3. The Annual Sessions, each lasting five months, commence on the 1st of March and the 1st of October, and end on the last day of July and the last day of February, respectively. Students can join the School at any time, the tickets running from date to date. The months of August and September, one week at Christmas, and one week at Easter or Whitsuntide, are Vacations. The classes meet every day *except Saturday*. Hours of Study: Day, 10 to 3; Evening, 7 to 9.

4. In connection with the Training School, and open to the public, separate classes are established for male and female students; the studies comprising Drawing, Painting, and Modelling, as applied to Ornament, the Figure, Landscape, and still-life.

FEES.

For classes studying for five whole days, including evenings: £5 for five months.
For three whole days, including evenings: £4 for five months.
For the half-day—morning, 10 to 1; or afternoon, 1 to 3: £4 for five months.
To all these classes there is an entrance fee of 10s.
Evening Classes: Male School: £2 per session.
Artisan Class: 10s. per session; 3s. per month.
Female School: £1 per session, three evenings a week.

No students can be admitted to these classes until they have passed an examination in Free-hand Drawing of the 2d Grade. Examinations of candidates will be held weekly, at the commencement of each session, and at frequent intervals throughout the year.

5. Students cannot join the School for a shorter term than *five* months, but the students who have already paid fees for five months may remain until the end of the scholastic year on payment of a proportional fee for each month unexpired up to the 31st of July in each year.

6. Classes for School-masters, School-mistresses, and Pupil-teachers of Elementary Schools meet on two evenings in each week. Fee 5s. for the session. Teachers in private schools or families may attend the day classes on payment of a fee of £1 per month.

7. The morning classes for Practical Geometry and Perspective are open to all students, but they may be attended independently of the general course on payment of a fee of £2 per session for those classes.

8. Students properly qualified have full access to the collections of the Museum and Library, either for consultation or copying, as well as to all the School Lectures of the Department.

9. A register of the students' attendance is kept, and may be consulted by parents and guardians.

Nothing can exceed the care and devotion with which the great work of South Kensington is carried on by both teachers and pupils. In walking through the rooms with the head-master I could only marvel at the indications unintentionally furnished by the pupils, from moment to moment, of his intimate knowledge of their work and their progress, however remote from such details he might be officially. In his room he keeps all the works sent in by the pupils in competition for the many valuable prizes offered by the school at each stage of progress, and these are preserved in large albums, each marked with the young artist's name, so that by looking through it we trace the unfolding in this or that direction of a human mind, from the first crude geometrical drawing to mastery of the finer strokes of form and color. The pupil applying for admission is not simply put in at one end of a machine-like system to be turned out at the other, but a specimen of his or her work is demanded, and a place assigned in accordance with it.

It was morally impressive to witness the large numbers of women who have here found a field for the cultivation of their powers. In one room—that of geometrical proportions—the students of both sexes are taught together, and no doubt the co-educational system will gradually creep from this to other classes, as it has to some extent done in University College and other institutions. But the museum is able to supply both schools with any quantity of models and aids. The young female artists have excited the admiration of their teachers and examiners by the remarkable perfection to which they carry ornamental designs, especially such as may be derived from flowers, fruits, and

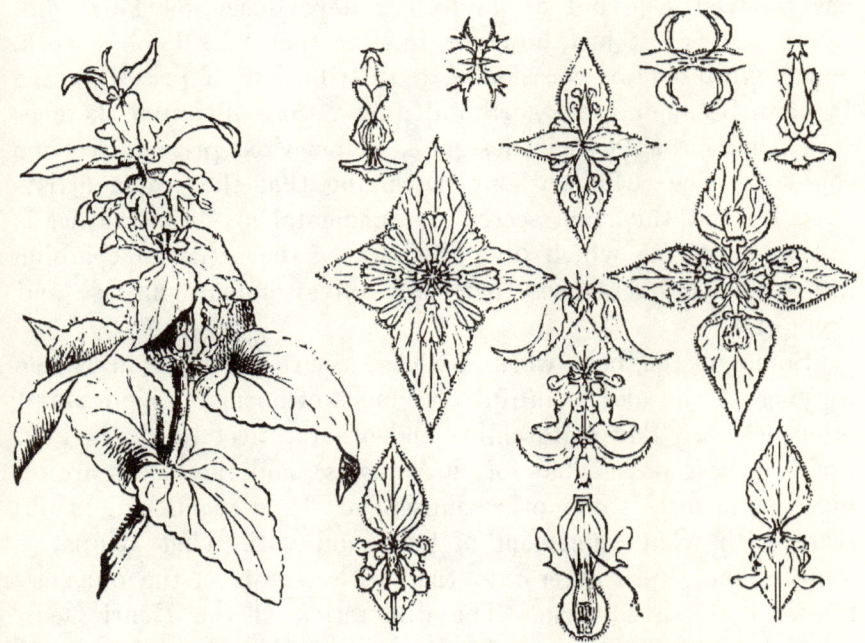

NETTLE IN ITS NATURAL STATE.   NETTLE IN GEOMETRICAL PROPORTIONS.

leaves. In one part of the museum there is a series of grottoes, filled with all manner of ferns and other plants, which serve the double purpose of adorning the room, from which they are seen through large glass doors, and of supplying subjects for the study of decorative foliation. They who see the beautiful combinations of these plants made in the training schools will discover that their previous acquaintance with some very common things has been very limited. In this study of the geometrical capacities of plants for decorative purposes the female pupils seem to excel. The exquisite art of one of them, Miss Louisa Poole, enables me to present an example of this kind of work, for which she recently received a gold medal. The subject of this very clever piece of combination is the common nettle; and, even without the beautiful colors with which Miss Poole's original work was rendered, these outlines she has drawn for me will perhaps enable the reader to understand the kind of work by which this school has relieved England of its former dependence on Paris and Lyons. It is but just, however, to state that Miss Poole's work, when exhibited, on occasion of a distribution of prizes by the Duke of Richmond, was surrounded by a score of similar sketches which had brought their designers well-merited prizes. No one could examine them without perceiving that the young artists have learned the main secret of ornamental art—that nature is but an alphabet, which it is the task of the artist to combine into words and sentences that shall convey human purpose and thought.

Some of the best work done at South Kensington is the copying of rare and beautiful specimens of ancient majolica and other wares. The Rothschilds and other collectors gladly lend their choicest possessions for this purpose, and the copies are of high value to this and other museums. It is wonderful to observe with what refinement of taste and with what sympathy some of the pupils enter into the subtle secrets of the old masters of decorative work. The illustration of the Henri Deux salt-cellar was made for me by Mr. William Broad, while a pupil at South Kensington, from a work sent in by him to the Examiners. The reproduction of Cherpentier's rich and delicate colors in this young artist's original work was exceedingly fine. His design of the top of the salt-cellar is given on the following page.

It is quite certain that a peculiar excellence has been given to the work of this institution by the atmosphere of general culture surrounding it. Each pupil works amidst the splendors of ancient art, amidst the shades of the great, and each lives in the presence of men who to-day best represent the accumulated knowledge of the world. The spirit tells more than the letter of instruction. Moreover, no art is here studied in isolation: each is studied along with literature and science; and, what is of great importance to thoroughness, all the arts are studied in connection with their own history. Through the literary works of such archæologists as William B. Scott, the ever-careful teaching of Thomas Armstrong and Mr. Sparkes, and the practical labors of such experts as Mr. Moody and Mr. Bowler, the pupil may study, by theory and experiment, the evolution by which his task has come to him, when and how great successes were attained, and so inherit the vital spirit which of old quickened the flowers of beauty by which he or she is at every moment surrounded. The pupil will realize here the immortality of good work. He will see that an old blacksmith, ordered to make iron grilles for Hampton Court garden, put such heart and soul into his work that his four pieces must now be brought hither as a monument of which Thor might be proud. Never was more beauty wrought in iron than

PLAN OF TOP OF HENRI DEUX SALT-CELLAR.

this by Huntington Shaw, of Nottingham, anno 1693. Under his hand rose, shamrock, and thistle have grown on the metal so tenderly that it would seem a breath might stir them, while from the Irish harp in the centre one might almost listen for Æolian strains. But that was done in a day when to work for a king was felt to be working for God. And all through this museum shines the great fact that the best work was never done merely for money, but for the altar, for love and loyalty. It is a Museum of Civilization, where each work is a heart. There sat a man doing his very best to advance the whole world; there marched a brave invader of Chaos and Disorder; a reason worked through him like that which turns a bit of mud into a lily. It is a supreme joy to trace these footprints of the universal Reason. A flute-key that wins one more soft note from the air; a pot flushed with some more intimate touch of the sunlight; an ornament which detaches a pure form from its perishable body—such things as these exhibit somewhat finer than themselves, namely, man elect still to carry on the ancient art which adorned the earth with grass and violet, and framed the star-gemmed sky and the spotted snake. The student shall also learn here the solidarity of genius. In distant regions of the world these men worked at their several tasks, sundered by land and sea, but here they are seen to have been members of one sacred guild, like that described of old: "They helped every one his neighbor; and every one said to his brother, Be of good courage. So the carpenter encouraged the goldsmith, and he that smootheth with the hammer him that smote the anvil, saying, It is ready for the soldering: and he fastened it with nails, that it should not be moved." From manifold regions of the world, through ages linked each to each by natural piety, their works have come here to unite in one mystical symphony of excellence. By the spirit that worked through them they are made members one of another. Some little time ago the Professor of Political Economy at Oxford formed a class of youths of both sexes, and said to them one day: "There are two great distinctions between man and the lower animals; one of them is the root of labor, the other is the root of civilization. What are they?" The first was soon explained; the root of labor is that the animal has only to seek his food to find it prepared for him, and his clothing is made for him by nature, whereas man must cook and modify his food, and make his clothing. The second puzzled all in the class except one young maid, who said: "The root of civilization is progressive desire. Give an animal all that satisfies its present want—good shelter and food enough—it will never be restless, nor show a further want; but satisfy man in any moment, he will want something better the next. This craving for the better and the best leads on to civilization." But it is the combination of these various lines of improvement which finally creates a civilization. Savages improve on their own roads, but the Kaffir never borrows for his own hut any advantage belonging to the hut of the Zulu, not more than the bee borrows for its cell a hint from the bird's nest. The savage has the root but not the flower of civilization. But then each civilization in turn is to a great extent special; the human race has a wider life, into which all separate streams of blood are poured, and all arts blend. By a higher law of evolution man's moral and intellectual powers are selected from the isolated tribes and nations through which they have for ages been distributed. In this our museum men are taken as varied pigments to make the study of Man.

> "Man, one harmonious soul of many a soul,
> Whose nature is its own divine control,
> Where all things flow to all. . . .
> Man, oh, not men! A chain of linked thought,
> Of love and might, to be divided not."

Of all countries America is that to which mankind must look for the fulfilment of those aspirations which are the creative force, carving on the world the ideals of poetry and art. Each fine work will reflect the culture of the race. Emerson has reminded us that for the best achievement we must have instead of the Working-man the Man working, and it were a pity if the great man's countrymen should not realize that whole work must be done by the whole man. In walking through the school at South Kensington once, I met a young lady who had passed several years in the schools at Philadelphia and the Cooper Institute, but had never found what she required for her training until she came here. The picture on her easel proved her to be an accomplished artist, and her experience appears to me worth mentioning. The school at Philadelphia, she said, was the best she had known anything of in the United States, but when she was there it lacked trained teachers. The teachers were artists in all but the art of teaching. She believed, however, that the Philadelphia school, if associated with a good collection, would turn out well. But of the Cooper Institute she was not so hopeful. It was rather too philanthropic to be a good school of art. The great aim was to qualify the pupils—girls particularly—to make money. The pupils are urged on to the paying work rather than to that which is excellent. It must be understood that these criticisms are here detached from this lady's pleasant plaudits to things in America other than its schools of design, her experience of which was that one with a high standard had no means of attaining it, while the other, with more resources, had a low standard and aim. This lady's experience has been several times confirmed by American artists with whom I have walked through the South Kensington Museum. One of the most eminent of them said: "What a revolution it would cause in American art to have some such museum as this in each large city! It would in each case draw around it an art community, and send out widening waves of taste and love of beauty through the country."

These expressions, however, were used ten years ago, and it may be hoped that to those now in the American institutions mentioned that may appear a dim past. Within that period my own visits to the chief schools of high art in New York have convinced me that their teaching is of the highest character, while the resources for culture of decorative art are slight.

If there be among the readers hereof one of those sensitive patriots who resent the idea of borrowing any ideas or methods from the Old World more modern than the Decalogue, I would submit even to him whether it be not less humiliating to import European experience than to export American brains. It is no dishonor for America to claim her inheritance from the past; it is no degradation to recognize what has been done as done, and not needing to be done over again; but it may well be pondered by the patriotic whether the Coming Artist will go abroad, or whether he shall find in his own country the resources essential to his culture and his finest fruit.

DECORATIVE ART AND ARCHITECTURE IN ENGLAND.

DECORATIVE ART AND ARCHITECTURE IN ENGLAND.

MICHAEL ANGELO was once commissioned to lead in the destruction of the beautiful villas around Florence. He of all men! The expelled Medici, now of papal dignity, were menacing the city. The first thought of the great artist was to save the Campanile, and he covered that noble work of Giotto with protecting wool-sacks. But the suburban villas must not stand to give aid to the enemy, and at word of command he started out, and for once the track of the great artist was indicated in the destruction instead of in the creation of beautiful things. But he came upon one house whose wall was covered with a beautiful fresco, and he had not the heart to destroy it; the soul of the artist held back the hand of the patriot, and in the field of desolation one mansion remained standing alone—saved by the protecting genius of Beauty.

It is but one incident in the long history of the career of Use and Beauty through the world, hand in hand, undivorceable. All our science is engaged in spelling out their story. Every spot of color on bird or insect it finds to be the trace of a utility. What weary struggles carried on through ages to mimic blossom and leaf, and so hide from pursuing foes! The same force works on when the art of man enters the arena for new creation. The thin and feeble blossom of the brier passes through all the phases of culture until it becomes the full rose of the horticulturist, like unto some little maiden's face for size and lustre, all by merest mercenary influence. Our fairest flowers have migrated from East to West, cherished and preserved for highest use as oracles and symbols of successive goddesses and saints, transplanted from temple courts to flourish under the holier chrism of convent gardens. Despite his proverb, man has painted the lily and adorned the rose, until we may almost say with the Persian Nizámi, "Every flower growing in the many-colored garden of the earth is a drop of blood from the heart of a man." Out of a dry and hard necessity comes still the beauty of the world. Behind our tinted Salviati glass, our painted Sèvres china and Minton majolica and shining silver plate, are the long rows of pallid faces inhaling poison in stifling rooms, breathing death that they may live. Sad experience is the prelude to each charming symphony. The noblest statues and paintings which the world cherishes were wrought in a "sad sincerity;" in the divine depths of sorrow were found the quarries from which emerged the Apollo Belvidere and the Laokoon; the blood of great hearts supplied the chief pigment of the Dresden Madonna and the Transfiguration; and the magnificent frescoes of Italian churches were born of the hopes and fears of millions, for whom they meant not picturesque beauty, but a world's redemption. Man in his best epochs of art has thus carried on the ancient creative power of Nature, giving her potential germs and forms a new blossoming under the heat of his never-ending battle of life. And where it is not thus impelled by nor surrendered to this utilitarian, this most real, force, what does Art amount to? Mere copying of works which denote that force in the past; mere Art Ritualism, crying to other ages, Give us of your oil, for our lamps are gone out!

If Michael Angelo could to-day be set on a work of general demolition in London, one may fear it would hardly require patriotism to encourage his zeal. Would he, in what the London *Times* once called "this our ugly but not altogether uncomfortable metropolis," have reached a single building which would have made him pause? Here and there he might meet one of those ancient mansions whose bricks have hardened into one solid stone that will stand, as Carlyle once said, "till Gabriel's trump blows it down;" but of the miles of modern houses in which—to remember the Chelsea sage again—"every brick is a lie," one may fancy that but few would be saved by any genius of Beauty.

And yet this is, after all, not so certain. That an artist filled with iconoclastic rage might quickly despatch most of the mansions and many of the churches of English suburbs, erected specially for beauty and effect, is quite probable; but there are a number of buildings built without reference to beauty which might perhaps have made Michael Angelo pause with a feeling not unrelated to admiration. If any one will stand beside the Thames River near Charing Cross and gaze for a while on the tremendous sections of the railway bridge there, at its huge iron supports and girders—if he will then go up on it and realize its vast breadth, see four trains passing each other, with room enough between, and room enough for the men and women moving to and fro on their own side-path—he will surely bear away an impression of grandeur. Nay, there will blend with it an impression of beauty also: there is no arch, no slightest foliation or other prettiness, not even a relief to the iron hue save the gilded heads of certain enormous rivets and the gilded monograms of the railway company fixed on the supports of the triple gas-lamps; the bridge is not even straight; and yet beauty there is, and it arises from two sources. The first is the beauty of adequacy for a purpose, involving at once strength and proportion, suggesting what the Greeks may have meant when, in their myth, they wedded Aphrodite to Hephaistos. The second is a beauty almost indescribable in physical terms, but resembling the simplicity which expresses character—the subtle charm playing unconsciously through eye and voice of even a homely man, who in word and act is content with the simple truth. In fact, the beauty of this Charing Cross bridge, which has least aimed at architectural effect among those spanning the Thames, is closely related to its ugliness. If any one find this assertion paradoxical, he shall at least find it not doubtful if he can and will do three things—read Oersted's chapter on "Ugliness in Nature," observe carefully Turner's "Rain, Wind, and Speed" (a railway train thundering over a viaduct through English rain and fog), and finally give twenty minutes to the bridge in question, especially taking care to pass beneath it on one of the small iron steamers (water omnibuses) that ply the river. When afterward he shall see the many ornaments of the present copied from the utilities of the past—the towers, steeples, cupolas, crenelles—and remember that they were constructed originally for landmarks, cross-bows, and the watches of war, he will acquire an imaginative respect for this unpretending product of the Iron Age. The same simple grandeur invests old Newgate Prison—perfect reality, entire adequacy for its purpose, a relation of every part to the end for which it was built, like the harmonies that make the lion. Did man forbear, it were by no means inconceivable that when Macaulay's artistic New Zealander came he might sit upon a broken column of St. Paul's to sketch the still strong, gray fortress of Newgate!

He who explores the cities of England to discover that kind of beauty in architecture which is familiar in other lands will not find it. In a late satire on the royal family published in London, *The Silliad*, the Queen is represented as reproaching her eldest son with not taking more after his father, and interesting himself in the industrial affairs of the country. The poor Prince of Wales can only reply, "I've not a model-farming soul." And a somewhat similar answer is all that England can return to the immeasurable scoldings poured out upon her because she cannot do the work of the old Italian and Dutch masters. But the time was when England had a reputation such as no other country possessed for just one thing—genuineness of work. It was almost proverbial in Europe to say that you could get pretty things in every capital on the Continent, but if you wanted a thing which would do what it professed to do—the knife that would cut, the carriage that would bear and wear—you must go to England for it. Nay, I remember in my boyhood in Virginia that the belief in the solid character of everything English was such, that even articles which could by no possible means have come from England were yet called "English" to enhance their value; not merely watches made in New England, but I have known American fanciers commend a bird unknown to England by calling it the "English mocking-bird!" All this was a droll re-appearance of the reputation which Eastern gold once had in England, the word "sterling" being a relic of "Easterling," as applied to the British pound of silver when represented in gold. But the most enthusiastic Briton must admit that the virtue of the "English" label has followed that of the "Easterling," and is now a mere survival. The absence of prettiness remains, but the old compensation of genuineness can no longer be claimed, or certainly not in the same general way. The genuine and thorough thing is now exceptional enough to strike one as almost ornamental. But still the word "solidity" has a meaning in Great Britain, and whenever Englishmen undertake to have anything done, their first effort is to have it substantial and useful. They may not get it, but that is what they pay for, and a real demand is likely in the long-run to overtake its real supply. It has already to some extent overtaken it, and that not alone in the great viaducts and railway bridges which the age of steam has called about it.

An age of municipal and civic development has found for the buildings it requires a representative architect in Mr. Waterhouse, who has erected most of the magnificent town-halls and court-houses of the great provincial cities. These vast, and in a certain sense beautiful, buildings are the only ones that can compare with the old cathedrals and castles of England, built with as serious a purpose as theirs, and with as physiognomical a relation to the age that produced them. Mr. Waterhouse takes the Gothic style for his basis, just as a pomoculturist might take a russet as the basis of the apple he means to produce, and, like him, modifies only in obedience to the fundamental law of the style he has selected. His Gothic building has in it nothing capricious or eccentric. So genuinely as, under change of conditions and needs, the bent and bound boughs were copied in the first pointed stone arch, even so, by lawful adaptation, may the window point become more obtuse or the lancets more lumi-

ASSIZE COURT, MANCHESTER.

nous; but the lesson of this style, which, above all others, has no part or trait not traceable to a use, is never lost, and the Gothic of Mr. Waterhouse is the natural evolution of that found in Westminster Abbey. In one of his buildings, and one of the best structures in the world, the Manchester Assize Court, I could discover but two things which appeared to me without special use or meaning. These were two small figures, a snail and a frog, carved in granite, sitting in the angles of a wall on each side of the main door-way. Of course these may not be mere *jeux;* they may have some connection with a previous bit of eccentricity in an older building (such as it is often desirable to copy and preserve for archæological reasons); but these two forms, each about as large as one's two fists, were the only things in the vast building which appeared "not to the point." In going over this building I speedily found that it would not do to pass anything, as the most casual-seeming bit of ornament was apt to possess a root in history. Thus the superstructure of the great portico at the entrance is supported by detached shafts of solid granite two feet in diameter, which stretch out into foliage as they meet the low roof; but on examination it is discovered that, framed in this foliage, are finely carved and most appropriate representations of ancient modes of punishment —persons undergoing the pillory or some ordeal, broken on the wheel, wearing the mask, or bridle, for scolds, and the rest. On the outside wall the decoration of the upper edge of a large corbel is twined about the words, "He shall judge thy people with righteousness, and thy poor with judgment." Over a gate leading to the judges' residence the tympanum of the gable is adorned with a fine mezzo-relievo of the Judgment of Solomon. On each side of the grand entrance are carved two chained dogs, imposing enough to be mythologically descended from Cerberus and Orthros themselves. There are but two figures on the outer walls, one of "Justice," another of "Mercy." The building is a parallelogram in form, with a frontage of 335 feet. Within is a grand hall 100 feet long, 50 feet wide, 75 feet high, with an open timber roof of eight carved bays, the principals having moulded brackets and ribs forming pointed arches, and the spandrels filled in with elegant tracery. Carved figures hold the chandeliers. Around this hall, which is for state receptions and banquets, run in ancient letters the words of the Great Charter: "Nullus liber homo capiatur vel imprisonetur aut disscisiatur de aliquo libero tenemento suo vel libertatibus vel liberis consuetudinibus suis, aut utlagetur aut exulet aut aliquo modo destruatur, nec super eum ibimus nec super eum mittemus, nisi per legale judicium parium suorum vel per legem terræ. Nulli vendemus nulli negabimus aut differemus rectum vel judiciam." This makes about as beautiful a cornice edging as can well be imagined. The last sentence is repeated on a stained window at the end of the hall:

<blockquote>
To none will we sell
To none will we deny
To none will we delay
Right or Justice.
</blockquote>

The subject of the window illustrates the history of the Great

MINTON TILE.

Charter — King John in the centre, and Archbishop Langton and Chief Baron Robert Fitzwalter on either side. There are three miles of corridors, all with a dado of tiles more than a yard deep, of a rich brown tint, and capped with a scroll made of lighter colors. On the whole, I can hardly express adequately my admiration of this superb building, the total cost of which was £130,000.

In the centre of Manchester the same architect has erected a larger building, a Town-hall, which cost £1,000,000. Rich and admirable as it is, it is not, on account of the crowding of houses around it, and the irregularity of the ground upon which it is built, so effective in appearance as the Assize Court. The interior decoration is remarkable for the beautiful variety of colors secured by a careful mingling of English, Scotch, and Irish granites grouped as double stems in the balustrade of a spiral stairway. The Irish granite is a bluish-gray, the Scotch has a faint red tint, and the English Shapfels has salmon-colored spars, which are as large as raisins. They all take a beautiful polish, and I think that for a large public building the effect is better than if they were marble.

Manchester has shown good sense and good taste in having employed Mr. Ford Madox Brown to paint six, at least, of the panels in the great hall of this Town-hall. These mural paintings are not surpassed by any recent work of the kind which I have seen. Mr. Madox Brown is pre-eminent for his archæological knowledge and poetic conceptions, and his genius has been at its best in these noble works. At the time of this writing three panels have been finished. The first represents the Romans building a fort at Mancenion (Manchester), anno 60. Agricola, Governor of Britain, is represented with a centurion beside him, examining a parchment plan of the Camp; a standard-bearer holds the silken Dragon-standard—emblem borrowed from the "barbarians"—which floats in the wind. The Legionaries are doing mason-work; Britons bear the stones and cement. Agricola's wife and little boy are in the scene. The second panel represents the Baptism of Edwin, at York, in the year 627. The artist follows the account of Bede, who says that a small wooden church was hastily erected for this purpose on the site where York Minster now stands, but has introduced a Roman mosaic floor. In his noble picture of Edwin he has been inspired by Wordsworth's sonnet, "Paulinus:"

> "Mark him, of shoulders curved, and stature tall,
> Black hair, and vivid eye, and meagre cheek,
> His prominent feature like an eagle's beak;
> A man whose aspect doth at once appall
> And strike with reverence."

The third panel is the Expulsion of the Danes from Manchester. One less acquainted than this artist with ancient fact might be surprised at the beardless, boyish appearance of the escaping Danes; but it is true that the Vikings began their adventures early—at the age of fifteen, it is said—and became respectable married men a few years later. The town-folk are hurling missiles at the retreating party, one of which—thrown by a young woman from a house—strikes down the "Raven" standard. Mr. Madox Brown's further designs include "The establishment of Flemish Weavers in Manchester, 1330;" "William Crabtree (draper, of Broughton, near Manchester) observing the transit of Venus, 1639;" and "The Decree Court Leet that all weights and measures are to be tested, 1566." No man is better able to invest with beauty these events connected with the history of Manchester. Mr. Madox Brown is using for these mural paintings the " Gambier-Parry " process. The medium consists of a mixture of wax, resin, and essential oil, with which the stucco of the wall is coated and the colors ground. Every color ever used with oil, water, or fresco is admissible with this medium; and the surface when dry is without shine, while yet the utmost luminosity pertaining to any other method is attainable with it. It seems likely to become the general mode in this climate, and has given equal satisfaction to Sir F. Leighton and Mr. Madox Brown.

One other of the immense buildings which have become so characteristic of the populous centres of England I must mention, namely, the new Midland Railway - station, at St. Pancras, in London. This is probably the finest railway - station in the world, and it is the chief work of Sir Gilbert Scott. It is a vast pile, of which every outward detail is graceful and substantial, its turrets and great clock-tower superb. This immense building conveys, however, an unpleasant impression of being out of place. It implies a park, or at least a larger and more picturesque space than the irregular and ugly one at King's Cross, to secure the perspective needed for any sight of it as a whole. Entering, we find ourselves beneath a vast span of iron and glass, almost like a sky. The front part of the building is a hotel. It has been decorated by Robert Sang, and furnished by Gillow, in the most expensive style, and certainly presents some rich interiors. The reading-room has green cloth-paper, and a ceiling gay with huge leaf frescoes; it is divided by a double arch with gilded architraves. The mantel-pieces are of dark marble, with two small pillars of yellow marble set on either side. The coffee-room has a general tone of drab, with touches of gold in the paper, and a sort of sarcophagus chimney - piece, surmounted by an antique mirror of bevelled glass. The sitting-room has red floral paper, and an imitation mosaic ceiling. One of the bedrooms which I visited had deep-green paper, with gold lines and spots, and bed-curtains somewhat similar. The furniture was of heavy oak, tastefully carved. The halls and corridors have a dado of fine dark - brown tiles, and bright fleur-de-lis paper above. All of which was rich, costly, and, with slight exceptions, by no means gaudy. Yet I could not altogether like it, or think the decorations entirely appropriate for a hotel. It looked as if there had been more exercise of ingenuity to find things costly than to find things beautiful. The *salon*, the reading-room, may naturally be made gorgeous, but the bedroom ought to be more quiet. One does not desire to sleep amid purple and gold. The traveller

KIDDERMINSTER CARPET—FERN DESIGN.

who needs rest may well spare these things—which, however, he knows will not spare him; for if there is gold paper on the wall, there will be gold paper in the bill.

For its purpose it would be difficult to fancy, impossible to find, a more complete structure than "The Criterion," which the great London caterers, Messrs. Spiers & Pond, have erected at Piccadilly Circus. This building includes social and private dining-rooms, room for *table d'hôte,* hall for public banquets and balls, restaurant, and buffet; and beneath all these a theatre large enough to entertain a thousand people. The architect, Mr. Thomas Verity, plainly had it in his mind to raise a great gastronomic temple, and when one enters the door, what he sees on every side is the apotheosis of eating. Through an archway we enter, and find ourselves amid the French Renaissance. The façade outside, and the door-way, with its glazed framing and superb bronze columns, make one feel that he is about to dine superbly. Really he does dine remarkably well, though the French Renaissance hardly extends to the culinary art of the establishment, for that would imply a revolution in the Briton's constitution. Mr. Wyon has placed some fair sculptures, the Seasons, etc., in the niches and on spandrels of the wall outside, but the inside decorations of Mr. Simpson are truly, in the words of Messrs. Spiers & Pond, "upon a scale which has hitherto never been attempted." The grand hall rises squarely through three stories to a light Mansard-roof, from which sun-burners blaze down at night, and outside of which is a promenade commanding a fine view of London. All of the sides of this grand and lofty hall are of tiles made for this establishment, and combining to form large pictures, the subjects of which were designed and painted by A. W. Coke. Over the right-hand door, leading to the restaurant, is a semi-classical scene of youth and maid by the sea-side gathering in fish; on the opposite side, over the door opening into the buffet, is a picture of two girls in a wheat field, where there is an apple-tree, the one attending to the sheaves, the other to the apples; around the lower hall are —still in tile mosaic—large figures of Euterpe and Terpsichore (for there will be music and dancing above), Pomona, Flora, Bacchus, and, of course, Diana, goddess of venison. The floor of the hall is as fine as any mosaic in London, and is adorned at the edges with the monograms of the firm. In the restaurant there are all manner of allegorical figures on the walls, the Seasons, and the genii which dig and delve and hunt, all with the object that humanity shall be fed. In the buffet there are charming tile pictures representing chubby boys and girls; one party up the tree gathering fruits, the other beneath catching the same and putting them into baskets; in each picture a different tree and fruit. On one side of the main stairway is the figure of a boy stealing up to a bird's nest, over which a bird hovers; opposite, the boy has the nest, the bird flies away. This device is not immoral; it means that plovers' eggs are on the bill of fare. One of the finest things in this staircase is an ebony hand-railing, three inches in diameter, with plated silver mountings. Also a very fine effect has been produced by framing the door-ways in

MINTON TILES FOR MANTEL.

white majolica, although greater simplicity in the designs than human faces festooned with flowers would, I suspect, have been

9

better. I must not omit to mention that the cornice inside the grand hall, at the top of the first and here floorless story, has the unique ornament of sentences from Shakspeare running all around the walls, with picturesque lettering:

> "None here, he hopes,
> In all this noble bevy, has brought with her
> One care abroad: he would have all as merry
> As first-good company, good wine, good welcome,
> Can make good people."
>
> "A good digestion to you all: and, once more,
> I shower a welcome on you;—Welcome all."

So it is that money enough enables common folk now to dine in palaces and enjoy banquets quite as royally served and surrounded as Bluff Harry offered to Cardinal Wolsey and the lords and ladies at the Presence Chamber in York Place. But even that monarch could not have entertained his guests so luxuriously in one particular as Messrs. Spiers & Pond theirs; for these, having dined, may pass through a door and descend by a stairway adorned with Muses and mirrors, and rich with floral clusters, to a theatre all glorious in blue and gold, cushioned chairs, boxes with curtains of yellow satin and lace, and a good drab background to set them off, and pass the rest of the evening in enjoyment of well-acted comedies or operettas.

So far as most of the hotels and restaurants of London are concerned, one may with satisfaction follow the advice of the Duke of Gloster to Anne, in the first act of *Richard III.:*

> "Leave these sad designs
> To him that hath more cause to be a mourner,
> And presently repair to Crosby Place."

For the old Gothic palace in the City, which Sir John Crosby built on a piece of land with one hundred and ten feet frontage, for which he paid a little over eleven pounds, which his widow sold to the duke who afterward became Richard III., and which in Shakspeare's time had fallen to the richest of Lord Mayors (Sir John Spencer), has now followed the course of so many royal buildings, and become the banqueting-hall of the public.

ALBERT MEMORIAL, HYDE PARK.

Crosby Hall is haunted by memories of the great. It gives flavor to everything one eats in it to know that it has been celebrated by Shakspeare, that from the year in which it was built (1466) it was associated with whatever has been most romantic

ALBERT MEMORIAL. EUROPE.

in the history of London. Here Sir John Rest was installed as Lord Mayor in the days (1516) when the Lord Mayor's Show meant something. The civic procession which accompanied him contained four giants, one unicorn, one dromedary, one camel, one ass, one dragon, six hobby-horses, and sixteen naked boys. Here resided Sir Thomas More, Under-treasurer and Lord High Chancellor of England. Here he wrote his best works, and received the visits of Henry VIII. Here Erasmus visited the author of *Utopia*, whose domestic life he described: " With him you might imagine yourself in the academy of Plato; but I should do in-

ALBERT MEMORIAL.—EAST FRONT. PAINTERS.

justice to his house by comparing it to the academy of Plato, where numbers and geometrical figures, and sometimes moral virtues, were the subjects of discussion; it would be more just to call it a school and an exercise of the Christian religion. All its inhabitants, male and female, applied their leisure to liberal studies and profitable reading, although piety was their first care. No wrangling, no idle word, was heard in it; every one did his duty with alacrity, and not without a temperate cheerfulness." In 1672 the hall was arranged for Non-conformist meetings. For ninety-seven years it was devoted to this purpose, and among those who preached here was Thomas Watson, who wrote the famous tract (*Heaven Taken by Storm*) which converted Colonel Gardiner. It is not wonderful that its old splendors then began to depart. The *Mercury* of May 23, 1678, advertised a sale at Crosby Hall, where would be disposed of, among other things, "tapestry hangings, a good chariot, and a black girl about fifteen years of age." Then it became the office of the old East India Company; next a literary and scientific institute; next a wholesale wine warehouse; and at length came into the hands of its present proprietors, who have restored it to its original purpose by making it a banqueting-hall. They have preserved it, and stained its windows with portraits and pictures representing all its history. The decorations are in perfect keeping with the beautiful Gothic style of the building, and the colors seem to have expanded on it as a flower on its stem. One seems to be dining here in an older Guildhall and at a daily Lord Mayor's banquet, with ancient Shaksperian characters for company. It is particularly entertaining to observe what a rich frieze can be secured for a hall in England by a skilful arrangement of the historic shields and coats of arms which belong to the country; while if some beautiful central figure on wall or glass is desired, it may be obtained in any one of the suggestive and mystical devices which are associated with the olden time—the boar, the lamb with its flag, and so on.

But neither the Criterion nor Crosby Hall furnishes, as I think, the same degree of beauty appropriate to dining-halls as may be found at the South Kensington Museum. Here one of the rooms was intrusted for decoration to Mr. Poynter, for a time President of the Art School there. He has made exquisite designs for the tiles of which the walls are altogether composed. The simple blue and white colors, and the purely decorative character of the figures thus made, make one almost regret that these figures are not Chinese instead of classic or allegorical, in which case one might eat with a feeling of comfortable seclusion in a china dish. The regular dining-room in the Museum was intrusted to Morris & Co., who have placed on the upper part of the walls a rich floral decoration of embossed plaster, colored (gray-green) by hand. The lower part of the wall, extending over two yards from the floor, consists of panels, on each of which is painted, on a gold ground, some allegorical figure. These figures represent the sun, the moon, and signs of the zodiac; they were designed by Burne Jones, and bear too

ALBERT MEMORIAL.—CONTINUATION OF EAST FRONT. PAINTERS.

much of that mystical light and expression which invest all forms and faces evoked by his magic touch to be gastronomically suggestive. In this respect neither Burne Jones nor the young artist (Murray) who painted his designs could rival the decorator of the Criterion; but one may dine at South Kensington amid one of the pleasantest little picture-galleries in existence. When Ralph Waldo Emerson was last in London, a poet who wished to give him a dinner conceived the happy thought of bringing him here, and the sage of Concord no doubt approximated his friend Alcott's ideal of "dining magnificently;" even the "bowls of sunshine" with which A. would replace wine were supplied by the rich stained windows of Morris, and by the brilliant white-and-gold of the restaurant which separates the two rooms so exquisitely decorated.

There is no doubt that the barbaric element in English taste received a fresh accession of vigor with the advent of the Georges to England. What it was capable of, and what it found pleasing to the aristocratic butterflies who flitted around him whom they adored as "the first gentleman in Europe," may be discovered in the Pavilion, at Brighton. That building may be regarded as the physiognomical monument of George IV. It is his cerebral interior projected into stone and decoration. The secret stairways and passages leading up to fictitious wardrobes, really doorways to rooms which his majesty desired to visit, represent the prince that sent horsemen to trample down laborers at Peterloo, whose only guilt was to discuss their wrongs; the bizarre carvings, which make fine stone look like terra-cotta, illustrate the fop who had come to prefer figment to fact. The interior decorations do not represent so well the monarch whom Thackeray analyzed, and found in his hands only a heap of pad, paint, gold-lace, but no man at all. Those frescoes were made during the first furor which occurred in England about Chinese and Japanese art; and, though ludicrously gorgeous, they are not without a certain interest, arising from the boundless freedom of their design and colors. How this can be it will be difficult for my reader to imagine, when he is told that the walls are covered with large dragons (life size, one might say, if dragons existed), serpents, wild cormorant-like birds, all having a grand field-day amid ladies and pleasure-grounds. The pillars are like barbers' poles, with the archæological serpent twined around each instead of the red stripe. The Pavilion is said to have found in Mr. P. T. Barnum its only admirer. English critics have been rather hard upon it. Sydney Smith said that the structure looked "as if the dome of St. Paul's had come down to Brighton and pupped." William Cobbett thought that "a good idea of the

ALBERT MEMORIAL—SOUTH FRONT. POETS AND MUSICIANS.

building might be formed by placing the pointed half of a large turnip upon the middle of a board, with four smaller ones at the corners." The main intent of the building is to imitate a Chinese pagoda, and it was with that aim that the Prince of Wales (for he seems to have been mainly his own architect) committed this enormity. Two years ago the British Association for the Advancement of Science gathered for its charming summer *séances* at Brighton, and the rooms of the Royal Pavilion were placed at their service. Never were the sessions of the Association so well housed, but it was amusing to witness the difficulty which even eminent savants had in the rivalry between the attractions of the wall-papers and the scientific papers. On the whole, it is to be feared that the grotesque ornaments left by the Regent carried the day. On one occasion, when a discussion occurred in the anthropological section on serpent-worshippers, the dragons and serpents on the wall were so appropriate that the room had the appearance of being frescoed for the archæological purposes of the day. But the ordinary contrast between the severe disquisitions of the scientific men and the luxuriant and barbaric colors and forms of the Pavilion was not so great as I witnessed recently in the same place. In the room which above all the rest might be regarded as the temple of vanity, a hundred ritualistic gentlemen and ladies had gathered to hold a prayer-meeting! In the evening there was a ball in the same room, and then it appeared plainly what had been the final cause of the Brighton Pavilion. I may add that the large building which George IV. erected for his stable, and whose roof is a vast dome, is now the chief concert-room of Brighton, and that another outlying building of the place is occupied by a fair picture-gallery, a good museum, and a capital library. Huish, in his *Memoirs of George IV.*, says: "Nothing could exceed the indignation of the people when the civil list came before Parliament, in May, 1816, and £50,000 were found to have been expended in furniture at Brighton, immediately after £534,000 had been voted for covering the excess of the civil list, occasioned entirely by the reckless extravagance of the Prince Regent, whose morning levees were not attended by men of science and of genius, who could have instilled into his mind wholesome notions of practical economy; but the tailor, the upholsterer, the jeweller, and the shoemaker were the regular attendants of his morning recreations." These mechanics were no doubt the worthiest folk who frequented the building they had made so fine, and probably most of them had to take their pay in royal smiles; but it would have relieved the indignant minds of the middle classes, who chiefly had to supply the exorbitant civil list, if they could have foreseen that their money was destined in the end to supply their favorite watering-place with an agreeable, instructive, and useful institution.

When the English people now look upon the Royal Albert Hall they are quite warranted in drawing pleasant conclusions as to the change which has come over the spirit of royalty since the Pavilion was erected. Here we have the real monument of the late Prince Consort, who, however he may be estimated, certainly did have the ambition to be associated with the progress

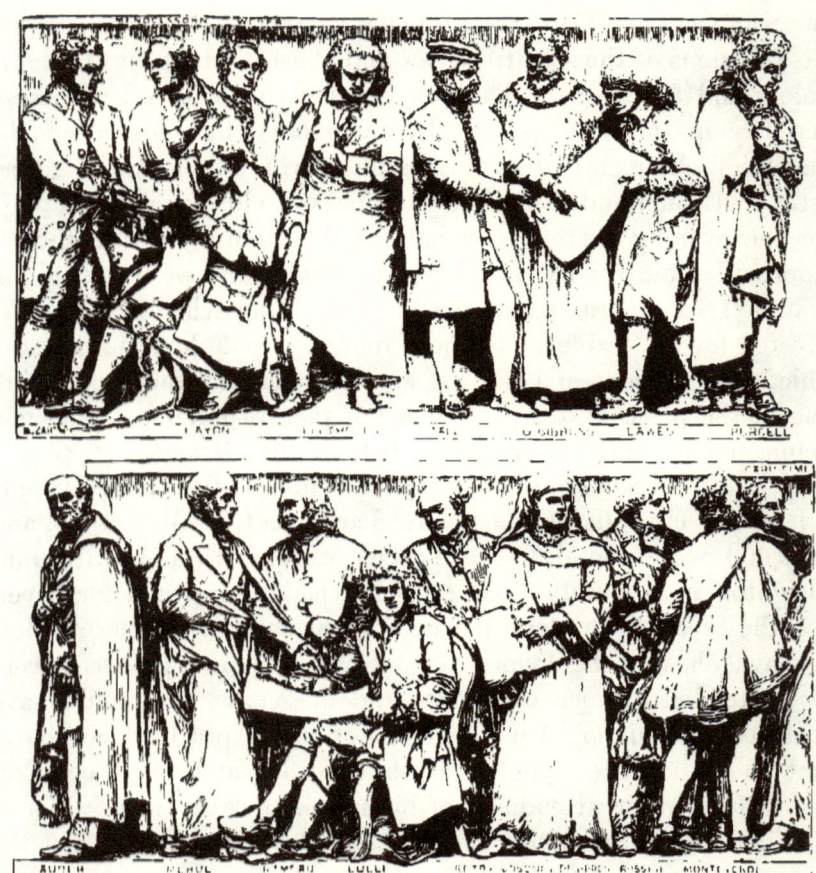

ALBERT MEMORIAL—CONTINUATION OF SOUTH FRONT. MUSICIANS.

of science and art in England. Since the erection of the Coliseum in Rome no building so stupendous and noble has been built as this. It is a pile worthy of Rome in its palmiest days; and, with its superb oval form, and external frieze and cornice moulded after the Elgin Marbles, devoted to international industrial and art exhibitions and to music, it stands as grandly amid the European civilization of to-day as the Parthenon stood in Greece. This palace of art, and the Albert monument in the park opposite, make the beauty-spot of London. The latter is beyond question the finest monumental structure in Europe. This afternoon, while the golden sunset of a balmy spring day was glorifying the sky, I walked to it, passing by the old Kensington Palace, where the little girl was informed that she was Queen of England who has since had her name associated with her country's longest period of peace and prosperity, passing beneath the ancient patriarchal trees and through the gardens beautified by flowers and plants from every region of the world, until at length I saw the spire of the monument shining like flame through the boughs. There against the clear, orange-tinted sky the monument stood forth, with its grand marbles at the four corners—Asia, with its genius mounted on a camel; America on her buffalo, Europe on her bull, Africa on her elephant, and each the centre of a representative group—and its noble reliefs and frescoes rising up to the winged angels at the top; and it appeared to me that every one of the one hundred and sixty-nine life-size portrait figures—the painters from Cimabue to Turner, the architects from Cheops to Gilbert Scott, who designed this monument; the sculptors from Chares to Thorwaldsen; nay, the very composers and poets from St. Ambrose to Rossini, from Homer to Goethe—had done something to raise this triumphal pile, about which their forms seem to move in stately procession. The architects and sculptors are the work of Philip; the poets, composers, and painters by Armstead; and while both have done admirably, it must be said that the reliefs by the latter are not surpassed by any modern sculpture. The group of Michael Angelo, Raphael, and Leonardo da Vinci, the kneeling form of Fra Angelico, are works such as can only be ascribed to that fine degree where intellect passes beyond ordinary analysis, and is called genius. Its central figure—Prince Albert—under the grand canopy, seems at first a conspicuous example of contemporary Hero-worship, showing that its highest and costliest homage is paid, not to any great Englishman—not to Shakspeare, not to Turner—but to a German, of whom it is certain that, had he not been a prince, he could never have excited so much attention as a hundred others of his fellow-men. At present the figure, not yet tested by time, is brassy enough, and is throned in brass; never was man more gilded over! But there is another side to this. The inscription runs: "Queen Victoria and her people to the memory of Albert, Prince Consort, as a tribute of their gratitude for a life devoted to the public good." The Prince received no such credit during his life; he got smirching enough then; but, if time tells as well on his statue as it has on his reputation, this figure will become increasingly worthy of its environment. Though no great man, he will sit there surrounded by the allegorical representations of art, commerce, and the various types of peaceful civilization, to which he did unquestionably devote himself. And it is something that the noblest monument in Europe, though better deserved by some who have no monument but their work, has at any rate been raised, not to any brilliant devastator of human homes, not to any royal oppressor or scheming diplomatist, but to an ordinary man, who used the position and means intrusted to him for the refinement and moral well-being of the country that adopted him. While the legend of one section of Europe is Napoleonic, there is some significance in the fact that Albert should have transmitted that of another section; and the essential —the moral—beauty of every admirable monument is thus not wanting to that which graces the largest and wealthiest city of the civilized world.

If the spirit of Prince Albert revisits the glimpses of Rotten Row, his once favorite haunt, he must long for the day when wind and weather shall have subdued some of the obtrusive glitter of his statue. It is too bad to be seen with too little light during life, and too much after death. It is sufficiently curious, while gazing on this overpowering mass of gilded metal, to remember what his private feelings were when some snobbish officials of London City proposed to erect a monument to him twenty-three years ago. The following letter, all the more creditable because necessarily private—the matter never having assumed such shape that he could speak of it publicly—was written at a time when its writer was believed by many to be the real instigator of the proposed monument to himself. It was addressed to Lord Granville, and is as follows:

"Windsor Castle, 3d November, 1853.

"My dear Lord Granville,—Many thanks for your letter, evincing such kind interest in what concerns me.

"I did not see the letter in the *Times*, but I read yesterday's leading article, which led me at once to considerations similar to those which struck you. Moreover, it is evident to me that the Lord Mayor started the plan chiefly as the means of bringing himself into notice, after other Mayors had gone to Paris, taken the lead in education, etc., and that the *Times* is attacking the plan chiefly to hit the Lord Mayor, as it had hit his predecessors. My unfortunate person will thus probably become their battle-ground; and, although the first article of the *Times* is civil, its music generally goes on crescendo, and the next may be purposely offensive, and meet with shouts of applause from a portion of the audience.

"Still, I do not see how I can, with any dignity or respect for myself, take notice of the squabble, and cry out for mercy, or to whom I could write such a letter as you suggest. I have never been consulted in any way in the matter, and the people have a perfect right to subscribe for and erect a monument in remembrance of the Great Exhibition; nor could I volunteer to say, 'You must not connect it in any way with me.'

"I can say, with perfect absence of humbug, that I would much rather not be made the prominent feature of such a monument, as it would both disturb my quiet rides in Rotten Row to see my own face staring at me, and if (as is very likely) it became an artistic monstrosity, like most of our monuments, it would upset my equanimity to be permanently ridiculed and laughed at in effigy.

"The *Times* argument, however, that it would be premature to place a statue to me, is of no great force in this instance, as I suppose it is not intended to recognize general merits in me, which ought yet to be proved, and might possibly be found wanting on longer acquaintance, but rather to commemorate the fact of the Exhibition of 1851, over which I presided; which fact will remain unaltered were I to turn out a Nero or a Caligula.

"As in all cases of doubt what to do it is generally safest to do nothing, I think it better to remain perfectly quiet at present. If I were officially consulted, I should say, 'Mark the corners of the building by permanent stones, with inscriptions containing ample records of the event, and give the surplus money to the erection of the museums of art and science.' Believe me, etc.,

"Albert."

Foley's statue would be nobler if the last paragraph of this letter could be read on it, and if he could have contrived some plan to let every observer know that the book held by the Prince is the Catalogue of the Great Exhibition of 1851.

There is some reason why the English artists should have done their best work upon the monument of Prince Albert. He may be regarded as the first man to teach this country that money might well be largely expended for the encouragement of fine art, and that it had artists capable of the best work, if the means were adequately supplied to them. He was the means of employing scores of fine brains that had otherwise been unable to make their mark on the country, and he extorted from a grumbling, shop-keeping public the splendors which now render the South Kensington Museum and its surrounding institutions an art university for the world. Very different have been the resources and rewards of the artists who have built and adorned the structures I have been mentioning from those which were alone available when the frescoes were placed in the corridors of the Houses of Parliament. Nevertheless, the Prince Consort himself had to be taught by a German artist to look around him for the ability which was needed for English work. When he was appointed the commissioner for the decoration of the Houses of Parliament (1841) he made overtures to Cornelius to come over and do the work. The German artist replied, "Why should you come to me when you have the man by your side—Dyce?" Dyce, who had studied at Rome with Cornelius and Overbeck, was then professor in the School of Design at Somerset House; but he was little known as an artist, and had not competed when designs for the decoration of Westminster Hall had been invited. The Prince Consort at once suggested to him that he should send in a design; and having too little notice to make a new one, he sent in a study he had made for a fresco for the Archbishop's palace at Lambeth. It was severely criticised, as too German, too papistical, etc.; but it was selected; and the result is the beautiful frescoes of the Baptism of Ethelbert, in the House of Lords, and of the Morte d'Arthur, in the Queen's robing-room. How slowly the ability of Dyce was recognized in England may be estimated by the fact that one of his most admired works—"Paul Preaching to the Gentiles"—now in the South Kensington Museum, was employed at an art exhibition in Manchester as background to an umbrella-stand!

But Prince Albert does not appear to have required a hint from Germany to appreciate the Scotch artist—son of a shoemaker—whose superior genius overshadowed that of his wealthy Irish brother. Already, while Dyce was as yet undiscovered,

Maclise had been appointed to set about those grand works which adorn the passage to the House of Commons. But the poor sums which were paid to both of these artists, and the grudging way in which they were dealt with, are now remembered only as a scandal. Dyce was sharply censured because he would not promise exact dates for the completion of his seven frescoes whose payment had been fixed by the Treasury at stated periods. Being rich, he offered to refund; but the Treasury, knowing that this would arouse some indignation, found it convenient to reply that "no precedent" could be found justifying its acceptance of his offer! Any one who looks upon Maclise's two pictures—"Trafalgar" and "Waterloo," the latter with three hundred figures, each perfect in line and expression — can but feel scandalized that Parliament proposed to pay him only £2000. Goaded by the outcry among the artists, it at length raised the sum to £10,000, but then grew sulky and cut off many of the commissions. In reality Maclise paid £30,000 for the honor of making those pictures. He gave the whole of four years to them at a time when his regular work never brought him less than £10,000 a year. When Cornelius passed through a South German town the ovation was such as no prince could command. When Maclise had completed his frescoes the artists of London presented him with a gold chalk-holder. The Prince Consort did all he could to raise an enthusiasm for decorative art in this country, and to raise the wages and the position of the artist and of the artisan, and he succeeded measurably; but time has sadly shown that he must have imported the climate of Italy rather than its schools to make this a country of beautiful frescoes. Although Cornelius magnanimously declined the overtures made to him, as above stated, in favor of Dyce, he consented to come to London and give advice concerning the proposed works. It was owing to him that frescoes were determined upon. He had seen the glory of the great frescoes of Munich; he could not see that in a few years they would be peeling off (as they are now) even there. Fortunately, Maclise resolved to put on his frescoes in silica, and they are yet fairly preserved; but all the pictures in the Houses of Parliament have had to be retouched from time to time, and the silica has such an attraction for the atmospheric moisture that the effect of the colors is frequently diminished. While it is thus manifest that the corroding damp of the English climate is hostile to mural ornamentation, and fatal to external frescoes, there is a steady increase of the desire for such things. This has been especially manifested among the English nobility, who have everything in the wide world that their hearts can desire, excepting only the climate that might comport with luxury and beauty.

That barbaric element in the English aristocracy, of which I have before spoken, which Mr. Matthew Arnold half likes while he impales its eccentricities, is constantly revealed in the contrasts between the baronial halls of England and the majority of the homes of the wealthy middle class. One may take as a specimen of the taste of the latter any one of the fine club buildings on or near Pall Mall. Here one feels that he is stepping on floors which the Pompeians would have thought somewhat sombre, but would have enjoyed, and amid walls and arches which they would have recognized as familiar, though strangely gloomy. The halls are large and spacious, rather costly than rich, built of purest granites and marbles of various hue; the reading, dining, and smoking rooms are comparatively quiet, and built with a view to comfort alone. The clubs represent the desire of gentlemen of means to pass their hours of leisure in palaces, and these are secured at an expenditure of less than a hundred pounds each per annum, even in the best of such institutions. But when one visits the castles of the nobility, such as are still inhabited, the fondness for color and romance is at once manifest. They love their rooms now blue, now green, and again rose-colored. They love classical frescoes—nude Muses, Graces, and Cupids chiefly—on the ceilings, and gay tints on the walls even of sleeping-rooms. In a word, my lords were sensational, and in some cases descended to the most vulgar tricks, as in the case which Wordsworth rebuked so sternly. On the occasion of a visit to Dunkeld the poet was taken into a room lined with mirrors, and where an artificial water-fall was set going by a spring being touched. The water-fall was reflected one way in the mirrors, but another way in the poet's face, and soon after in his rebuke of such mimicry of Nature:

> "Ever averse to pantomime,
> Thee neither do they know, nor us
> Thy servants, who can trifle so."

But what could come of a generation trained by the royal standard which thought it beautiful to tie oranges bought in Covent Garden Market on the twigs of trees at Hampton Court for a garden party? The mansions of the nobility are still really the most tawdry and inartistic in their decorations of any class that have attempted decorations—mere blazings of white-and-gold; but there is an increasing number of exceptions, represented especially by some ancient families which have manifested a laudable desire to have their halls painted with pictures of legends or historical events connected with their neighborhood or their ancestors. Mr. William B. Scott, artist and poet, who has done excellent mural work of this character, has, I believe, fairly persuaded both the aristocracy and the artists of England that they cannot have Italian frescoes in this country, and must depend upon mural painting. In exhibiting specimens of his own excellent mural painting, before the Institute of British Architects, Mr. Scott made some interesting remarks on fresco. "In Italy," he said, "the reign of fresco was a little more than a century in length. All the earlier works remaining are in tempera. Not many years ago it was not unusual to hear people talk of all early Italian wall paintings as fresco, but it is quite certain no such thing exists; the earlier frescoes, such as Mantegna's works, in the Eremitani Chapel, in Milan, are

SPANDREL PICTURE.

miserable ruins; while the tempera pictures of Giotto, a century and a half older, in the Arena Chapel, in Padua, for example, are perfect. How, then, did it come about that fresco, which died out in Italy very shortly after Michael Angelo finished the Capella Sistini, had a revival in this nineteenth century in Munich and London? A very short narrative of the circumstances attending this revival will, I think, be enough. The associated body of young German students assembled in Rome in the beginning of this century aspired to better things than they found existing in the lifeless art about them. They reverted to the study of earlier art—to the actual reproduction of former art. They were also pietists—at least the two leaders, Overbeck and Cornelius; they found that their patron saint, Fra Angelico, painted in fresco; they found also that all the mythological, anti-religious pictures of the Bolognese school and later period were in oil: they determined on the revival of fresco. King Ludwig seconded them, and furnished an ample field for their success. The misfortune was, they did not go back far enough; they were self-denying men, and even the hardships and difficulties of fresco had attractions for them. It was like a revival of Tudor in mistake for a revival of the best period of Pointed architecture. Several English artists living in Rome, after the great success of the first very able works of these revivalists—my brother, David Scott, of Edinburgh, and William Dyce, for example—were smitten with the same feeling."

Some eight years ago I had the pleasure of seeing the mural paintings with which Mr. W. B. Scott has decorated Sir Walter Trevelyan's house, at Wallington, in Northumberland. No person could have been more appropriately selected for the work than Mr. Scott, who passed much of his early life in that region, and has written such beautiful poems upon its ancient legends. The first (ground-floor) series of paintings is on panels, enclosed between pilasters supporting arches; and a second is on the spandrels above the arches, in a corridor leading to the bedrooms, on the upper floor. The mansion is near the ancient Scottish Border, so haunted by romance, and near it may still be seen the remains of the ancient Roman Wall. In four of the panels the subjects are (1) the building of the Roman Wall; (2) King Egfrid offering the bishopric of Hexham to Cuthbert, hermit on Farne Island; (3) a descent of the Danes on the coast; (4) death of the Venerable Bede. On the opposite side are later subjects, but equally related to the same region of country: (1) "The Spur in the Dish"—the sign to the moss-trooper that the larder is empty; (2) Bernard Gilpin taking down the gage of battle in Rothbury Church; (3) Grace Darling and her father saving the shipwrecked crew; (4) "Iron and Coal"—the industry of the Tyne. The pilasters and the arcaded ends are also slightly decorated with foliage. The pictures on the spandrels are a series of eighteen on the old Border ballad of *Chevy Chase*. They are full of spirit, and their rich colors are like bursts of sunset along the ancient corridor. So much, indeed, depends on this color that it is impossible to convey the artist's idea of mural painting by a woodcut. Nevertheless, I must confide to the imagination of my reader one characteristic design (page 147), "Women looking out for their Husbands and Brothers after the Battle of Chevy Chase."

For his decoration of Penkill Castle, Ayrshire, Mr. Scott appropriately selected the old Scottish poem of *The King's Quair*, or book (*cahier*, or quire, of paper), said to have been written by James of Scotland when a prisoner at Windsor, in 1420, on his love for Jane, granddaughter of John of Gaunt. The first picture shows the king in prison, turning from his reading for his pen. According to the canto in which the king describes his rising with the matin bell, there is pictured the bell, the warder, the night-watch going home, etc. In the second picture he looks from his window, and sees the fairest of womankind listening to the birds in the terraced garden. She has with her two maids and a little dog. Cupid—the Cupid of early art, a sort of pretty page—shoots at the king from behind a hedge. The third picture represents the royal poet's dream, in which Master Cupid descends from the starry sphere to carry him away to the court of Venus, to obtain her assistance. These three pictures run along a flight of stairs, and the series is taken up with the next flight. In the fourth picture the poet finds all the lovers of history at the shrine of Venus. James prays on his knees to her, but she sends him to Dame Minerva's court of wisdom for advice. Then we have the poet at the court of Minerva; next Lady Jane sending off the carrier-pigeon; and finally the royal poet receiving it. It requires but little reflection for any one to realize that to an ancient baronial castle such a series of paintings as this would be as the breathing of a soul beneath its gray ribs of rock. It must be mainly for the want of such pictures in them that servant-maids and children so often imagine ghosts rustling along old corridors and haunting antique stairways.

The castle of the Earl of Durham is graced by a fine stained window, illustrating the legend belonging to it of the slaying of the great worm, or dragon, by the Knight of Lambton; and the similar legend of Moore Hall is finely told in that mansion by the art of Professor Poynter. The last, however, is simply on canvas, and appeared as a large framed painting at the Royal Academy. It is, of course, necessary that a house should be very large and stately to bear mural paintings. The painting of panels is, indeed, becoming common in old houses which are well wainscoted, but as a general thing it is confined to the doors of more modern dwellings. However, a very fine effect has been produced in the dining-room of Mr. Birket Foster, at Witley, in Surrey, by inserting in the wall around the room a continuous painting by Burne Jones representing the legend of St. George and the Dragon. The stained glass which Morris & Co. have placed in the landing of the staircase, in the same beautiful residence, shows also that even a cottage-mansion of moderate size admits of a great deal more decorative color than is ordinarily supposed.

In passing from the consideration of works of a public and semi-public character I cannot refrain from paying some tribute to the most influential decorative artist whom England has produced, and whose death in April, 1874, all lovers of beauty are still mourning. Mr. Owen Jones carried into decorative art that spirit of archæological accuracy — one might almost say that profound scholarship — which was brought into pictorial art by Delaroche in France, Baron Wappers in Belgium, and Maclise in England. It is said that there was but one thing in England which the Shah of Persia wished to carry back with him to his palace — the Alhambra rooms, at the Crystal Palace; but of all their possessions, in the way of art, there is hardly one that the London people would so unwillingly part with. Yet it is probable that as little as the Shah the thousands who every week find in those rooms their *châteaux en Espagne* realize what it really cost to put them there. Mr. Owen Jones had passed his youth and his early manhood journeying, both personally and mentally, on the track of the race to which his fine culture belonged: he had studied the mystical figures and lines of Egyptian temples; he had pondered the principles by which reason and truth find expression in stone amid the ruins of Greece; he had learned the secrets of simplicity and grandeur in Rome, where were poured the converging streams of beauty from many tribes, each bearing its freight of faith and aspiration, to be deposited in marbles and monuments which are the gospels and bibles of a primitive world. By this path, which meant for him a growing culture, he came to dwell on the heights of Granada, as the recluse and devotee of Beauty, and when he thence returned to his native land he brought with him a new era. He expended a fortune on the grand folio of colored drawings of the Alhambra, which brought him no return, but a single copy of which is now a collector's treasure. When proposals were being received for the decoration of the glass palace of the International Exhibition of 1851, Mr. Owen Jones offered to Prince Albert and the Royal Commissioners his plans. The Prince held out against them for some time; but the fascination was on him, and again and again he returned to the exquisite designs, until he surrendered to their charm. He selected Owen Jones with some tremor, but every year since the Palace has been transferred to Sydenham has shown that it was a felicitous incident of his life to have encountered the right man for a task which was to be of far more permanent importance than he supposed. Since then Mr. Owen

Jones has not only given the large interiors of various great business establishments that beauty which makes many of them worthy of study and admiration, but he has won for himself and his country the highest honors of the three great Continental Exhibitions. It was with some amazement that the world found itself pointed to England as the leader in decorative art by the French Exposition of 1867. "It requires," said the official catalogue of that exposition, " but a slight insight into modern domestic life in England to perceive how great a change has taken place within the last ten or fifteen years in the internal embellishment of the dwelling-houses of the upper and middle classes of society; and there can be little doubt that the extension of art education will lead still farther to the production and appreciation of articles which combine the three requisites of fitness of purpose, beauty of design and ornament, and excellence of workmanship." It might be supposed by those who have not seen this master's work that it consisted merely in clever imitations of the Moorish and other designs with which his name is associated; but, on the contrary, his chief excellence was, that he showed how the ideas and principles which underlie the great works of the past were capable of being led out into new forms and adaptations. In taking the chair at the Society of Arts, in 1851, on the occasion of a lecture on the arts and manufactures of India, by Professor Royle, Mr. Owen Jones, having accorded superiority to the Indian and Tunisian articles in the Exhibition of that year over all contributed by Europe, added: "Many of these specimens have been purchased by government for the use of the School of Design, and will, no doubt, be extensively circulated throughout the country. But it is to be hoped that they will do more than merely teach us to copy the Indian style. If they only led to the origination of an Indian style, I should think their influence only hurtful. The time has arrived when it is generally felt that a change must take place, and we must get rid of the causes of obstruction to the art of design which exist in this country."

The *Daily News*, in an editorial article on the death of Owen Jones, said: "It was to bring the beautiful in form and color home to the household, and to mingle its subtle influences with the whole frame-work of social and family life, that the great designer we are lamenting labored all his life with the

OWEN JONES.

patient, unselfish enthusiasm of one to whom, though full of the keenest sympathy with all the great historic movements and events of his time, his art was his life."

The devotion of such a scholar and refined gentleman as Owen Jones to decorative art has helped to make an era in that kind of work. Before that it suffered in England from being regarded as a sort of upholstery, implying neither talent nor culture. Some gentlemen of culture and wealth recognized the genius of Mr. Owen Jones at a time when the Prince Consort was still inclined to regard him as a superior kind of upholsterer or house-painter, among whom must be especially mentioned Mr. Alfred Morrison, well known for his antiquarian and numismatical accomplishments. His residence in Carlton House Terrace is the truest monument of the genius of Owen Jones, and it is a work which need fear no comparison with any other, of whatever age or country. It makes the chief palaces of Northern Europe vulgar. Sádi tells us of one recovering from an ecstasy, who said he had been in a divine garden, where he had gathered flowers to bring to his friends; the odor of the flowers so overcame him that he let fall the skirt of his dress, and the flowers were lost. Some such account one must needs give of a visit to Mr. Morrison's house. A thousand of the touches, the felicities, which combine to produce the happiest effects in this mansion, can by no means be conveyed from the place where they would appear to have grown. I will only mention a few suggestive features of this system of decoration.

The house is one of those large, square, lead-colored buildings, of which so many thousands exist in London, that any one passing by would pronounce characteristically characterless. It repeats the apparent determination of ages that there shall be no external architectural beauty in London. Height, breadth, massiveness of portal, all declare that he who resides here has not dispensed with architecture because he could not command it. In other climes this gentleman is dwelling behind carved porticos of marble and pillars of porphyry; but here the cloud and sky have commanded him to build a blank fortress, and find his marble and porphyry inside of it. Pass through this heavy doorway, and in an instant every fair clime surrounds you, every region lavishes its sentiment; you are the heir of all the ages. Entering a room for reading and writing, near the door, we are conscious of a certain warmth of reception even from the walls. They are of silk, made in Lyons, after a design by Owen Jones.

The shade and lustre are changeable, but the prevailing color dark red. The design is as if an endless series of the most graceful amphoræ had suddenly outlined themselves, and the lines had taken to budding off into little branches. The surface is Persian, and the whole sentiment of the room is Oriental, without having in it a single instance where Oriental work has been copied. The carpet is Persian, but the design is by Owen Jones, the most noticeable figure being the crossed squares, making a star-shape to match a similar one on the coffered ceiling. This tapestry of silk starts a theme, so to say, which is carried, with harmonious variations, throughout the building, expanding in the larger rooms, until it recalls every variety of Etruscan shape, and taking on the most beautiful colors. There is a Blue Room, a Pink Room, a Yellow Room; yet in no case is there anything "loud" or garish in the tints. The ceiling of the reading-room is somewhat after the fashion of the best Italian work of four centuries ago—a kind of moulding in deep relief, which probably ceased to be much used because it was found difficult to make it without incurring the danger of its falling, so great would be the weight. But Owen Jones invented something which he called "fibrous plaster," by which the most heavily coffered ceilings can be made with perfect security. It consists in first making the shapes to be used in wood; the wood is then covered with canvas, and this canvas is covered with repeated coats of the finest plaster, which is rubbed down into any mouldings required, and painted. The coffers here are star-shaped, and in each an inverted convoluted shell of gold. It is an indication of how finely the decorator has blended Oriental lustres and classic designs that the various antique objects and fine metal-work, done by the best Spanish, Italian, and Viennese workmen, after classic models, everywhere set about the rooms, have an easily recognizable relationship with the scrolls and forms on carpets, ceilings, and walls.

But neither the Lyons silk nor the Persian carpets can be pronounced unique in the same sense as the wonderful use made of various woods in this house. In the dado, jambs, chair-boarding, we find no carved work, but simply the most exquisite combinations of ebonized and many-colored woods. Some of these, as the Indian holly, are so fine that the grain is invisible to the closest inspection. Other woods are so soft and beautiful that they have the surface of petals. Trees belonging to every land and clime of the earth have sent here their hearts, and, without a particle of pigment being used on any one of them, they gather to form rosettes on the chimney-pieces, cappings for the dados, and finest featherings around the doors — white, golden, red, cream-colored, brown, and these of every shade. The tables and chairs of several rooms are of this tarsia-work of forms untouched by staining or by metal.

In the library the book-shelves, which do the duty of a dado around the room, have alternate doors of glass and wood, and the latter are adorned with a foliation, over two feet high, growing from the bottom of the panel and leafing out at the top, which cannot be surpassed by any ancient marquetry. Above these shelves the green and gold lustres of the wall rise to a cone, which has the appearance of a blue and gold enamel, above which is an early Tudor ceiling of checker pattern, between reliefs of a large star with four shadings of different colors, or star within star, golden, dark, and white. The chimney-piece here may be regarded as a large arched cabinet, with fire-grate beneath, having two wings, in which are contained specimens of porcelain from Persia and Cashmere, which, old as they are, have an appearance of having been designed by the decorator of the room, who certainly never saw them until they came into the harmony he had prepared for them.

The drawing-room, whose windows overlook St. James's Park, is a very large apartment, whose division, if it ever had any, has disappeared, giving an unbroken range to the eye, which, whether it takes in the whole effect or pauses to examine a detail, is simply satisfied. The fretted ceiling; the frieze of damask picked out with gold; the tarsia dado, a necklace surrounding the room; the chimney-pieces, one of which Lepec of Paris was two years in making — they are all fine without frivolity, cheerful without fussiness. One mantel-piece reminded me of what Baron Rothschild is said to have remarked once, when a fop was displaying his malachite shirt-studs, "Very pretty; I have a mantel-piece of it at home." Some of the incised ornaments here are gems indeed, but in no case have they the appearance of being set there for their costliness; they are all parts of the general artistic work. One of the best features of this drawing-room is, that it is not "stuffed" with things. The objects in it are comparatively few, yet they are sufficient in number and variety; and being beautiful and interesting, one can look at each without being bewildered, as in some houses, where an idea seems to prevail that the model for a reception-room is a museum.

Mr. Morrison is a strenuous opponent of the general belief that the arts are deteriorating. He believes that as good work of any kind whatsoever can be done now as in any other age of the world, if one will only look carefully after the men who can do it. His experience has certainly been fortunate in discovering those who are able to make entirely original designs, and yet conceived in a purely artistic spirit; but then he has had all Europe at his command. The best metal-workers he has found in Spain and Vienna. In the former country he found out Zouloaga, a workman residing in the little town of Eybar, and from him has obtained chased and engraved metal-work such as almost any of our connoisseurs would be apt to date before the Renaissance on a cursory glance. One piece of work by Zouloaga is in the drawing-room—a large coffer, nine feet by three, covered with all manner of figures and scrolls in iron, wrought in relief, and with a finish which would have made Andre Buhl himself rejoice that his own fine cabinet (of which Mr. Morrison is the fortunate possessor) should have found a place under the same roof with that of the Spaniard. Mr. Morrison told me that he felt sure the man could do a fine piece of work, if encouraged, so he advanced him a thousand pounds, and told him to begin something on that. Zouloaga worked at the coffer for four years, and its owner saw at once that he had but paid an instalment of the real value of this marvellous work.

But though Mr. Morrison has had to go to Spain for ornamented metal-work, to Paris for his mantel-pieces, to Lyons for his silk, he has found that in no other country than his own was he able to secure the best wood-work. It may be, indeed, that if his desire had been for the most perfect carving, he might not have had the satisfaction of obtaining it in his own country— though some of the workers that Mr. George Aitchison appears to have got hold of may render even that doubtful. But in pursuing inquiries as to the means by which the exceedingly bold designs of Owen Jones for ornamentation with the colors of woods could be carried out (and the inquiries were not confined to this country), Mr. Morrison found that no house out of London was prepared to undertake a task that necessitated importations of select woods from all parts of the world. In Mr. Forster Graham, Owen Jones found a man able to enter into his ideas and to give practical effect to them. Indeed, the famous architect and decorator acknowledged his indebtedness to Mr. Graham for some effective suggestions for the improvement of the original designs. Those who know Mr. Morrison will easily understand that he too was by no means a mere by-stander while the work was going on. At any rate, he may now rejoice in having secured a home that has converted some portion of his wealth into a more real value. For there is nothing in this house not harmonious with its purpose. Every chair is as philosophically as it is beautifully constructed, and nearly every one is different from the other—one suggesting the perforated chairs of the Delhi palaces, and another the old Saxon throne in Westminster Abbey. It is related of a sensible and busy banker that, on being visited by some one, he said, "I have a line or two to write; pray take a chair." "Do you know who I am, sir?" said the visitor, haughtily. "I am the Envoy Extraordinary of ———." "Oh, are you?" said the banker; "then pray take two chairs!" This little story occurred to me as I was looking upon Mr. Morrison's chairs, and I fancied the Envoy Extraordinary, if asked to take one, would probably have considered it as a significant mark of respect.

There is no sham in this house—no wood pretending to be metal, and no iron affecting to be marble. As each particle of a rose under the microscope has the rose's beauty, so here each part of the mansion bears witness to the care and taste with which the whole is constructed—the table-leg as truly as the Lepec mantel-piece. We may ascend the magnificent stairway, past the globes of light upheld by bronze candelabra rising seven feet from the floor, and as we go from story to story find good, painstaking work meeting us everywhere—in the bedrooms, the nursery, the closets—some of the best ornamentation in the house being a pale blue-and-gold scroll surrounding the skylight at its top.

It is a pleasure to know that decorative skill has not passed away with Owen Jones. The house of Frederick Lehmann, Esq., in Berkeley Square, is the *chef-d'œuvre* of Mr. George Aitchison, one of the most celebrated architects and decorators in England, who has made the most of very favorable conditions, has called to his aid congenial artists and carvers, and has completed rooms which one would fain see themselves hung upon the walls of the Royal Academy, and not merely the designs of some of them, which were, indeed, exhibited there. The house is ancient, and, though not very large, built liberally and substantially, evidently in the days when Berkeley Square was near enough to "the country" for space to be of less consideration than now. In the course of the recent improvements there was found behind an old chimney-piece a playing-card, upon the back of which is written an invitation from a Mrs. Murray to Lady Talbot to pass the evening at her house; and Mr. De la Rue declares that no card of a similar character has been manufactured for a hundred and fifty years. Even farther back in time than that we may safely place the old-fashioned, nearly square hall—about twenty feet by seventeen—which is at once hall and vestibule. It contains tables, cabinets, and a stand for flowers, and the modern decoration sympathizes with what appears to have been the old idea of a vestibule—a sheltered cortile. The general tint is a very pale green, the surface-panelling large, and ornamented with stems starting from a common root and ending each in cones. The stems and cones curve toward each other, and form a sort of circular grouping. A door on the left introduces us to the library, whose walls are shelves of richly carved walnut, above which is a dark leather frieze, which elegantly sets off the treasures of ancient pottery and other antique objects which make the interesting finish of the well-stored bookshelves all the way around the room. At a certain point the books prove to be dummies, an unsuspected little door flying open at a touch and revealing a lavatory. In this library, where startling effects of any kind would be out of place, there are no plays of color, but ample light falling upon the exquisitely carved table for writing in the centre, which is the most remarkable for its conveniences and contrivances that I have ever seen.

Ascending to the drawing-rooms, we enter first a small apartment, whose floriated ceiling gives the effect of a bower. Between this and the golden cornice is a cove of inlaid gold, upon which are traced leaves of wistaria, interspersed with light pink clusters of the phlox. The chief ornament is a large cabinet, reaching nearly to the cornice — ebony and ivory — recently brought from the Vienna Exhibition: it contains specimens of Eastern porcelain and various curiosities collected by Mr. Lehmann, who would appear to have voyaged around the world and found relics of all civilizations and all the ages of art. This, however, is but an anteroom to the chief drawing-room, with which it communicates by a large double sliding-door. This door and another like it which admits to the dining-room are truly superb. They have a frame of ebonized wood, enclosing panels of finest-grained amboyna. The ebonized wood is foliated with gold, and the long central panels are adorned with ovals of olive-colored Wedgwood ware, presenting classical figures. The smaller panels above and below have at their centres squares of the same. Each door has a capping of gold floriation and a draping of French embroidered silk, at once heavy and delicate, like tapestry. The walls are of a dark reddish-brown color, arranged in large panels (from floor to cornice), enclosed by a fine painted edging. This background elegantly sets off the pictures, which are all excellent, some of them being among the best water-colors of Turner. The ornament which chiefly strikes the eye in this room is a matchless frieze, painted by the eminent artist Albert Moore, the design being peacocks, their long trains in repose. The cornice above this is of the egg-pattern, with a fretting above. The ceiling is, in a manner, panelled; that is, it has on each side stiles or beams crossing each other, making the large central space and the side spaces almost deep enough to be called coffered. These crossbeams are finely feathered with gold, and the interspaces are adorned with curved boughs, which have small pointed leaves terminating in round decorative flowers. The fireside of this room is highly ornamented. The grate is antique in general appearance, but novel in structure; the silver owls (life-size) sitting on either end of the fender-bar, and the old brass mountings of the fire-dogs, have come from the past to guard a grate which slides backward and forward as the regulation of the heat given out may require. The tiles are representations of six varieties of humming-birds, a paroquet, a sun-bird, and several other feathered beauties. Near by is a folding screen of brilliant Japanese silk. The room is covered to the border of the parquetage with a bright Persian carpet. In the dining-room the original ceiling, with dark oak reliefs (curved), has been retained—not happily, I am afraid, such ceilings always absorbing too much light. Mr. Aitchison has given the spaces a luminous decoration, but nevertheless the dark wood-work above can only be retained by the use of a corresponding shade in the furniture. This furniture is of rare beauty. The sideboard is most delicately carved, and the serving-table inlaid with medallions of ivory, the designs of which, by Albert Moore, represent various animals and fruits suggestive of the uses of the room. There is a chimney-piece of ancient work—ebony, with side pillars and excellent gold settings; but a comparison of this bit of last century work with the furniture recently made is likely to raise a question in the minds of those conservatives who insist that the making of beautiful things is a lost art. It is a pleasure to find hung in a room where each ob-

EBONY SERVING-TABLE, MR. LEHMANN'S HOUSE.

ject bears the trace of really fine art that portrait which has long been acknowledged to be the ablest work of Millais, representing Mr. Lehmann's little daughter seated upon a Minton garden-seat on a lawn. When this picture was exhibited at the Royal Academy, a few years ago, a writer in the *Fortnightly Review* pronounced it the work which, among modern English productions, most recalled the peculiar vitality and sentiment which have given the old masters their fame. I had the pleasure of seeing the little lady at that time in her boudoir, to make which beautiful Mr. Aitchison appears to have put forth his talent as earnestly as Mr. Millais to paint her picture. A blue border encloses the large panels of the walls, on which are *fleur-de-lis* spots, and a bittern at each panel centre. The frieze is painted in graceful floriations of lemons, and the cove above is adorned with balsam and jasmine. The apartments of Miss Lehmann, thus tenderly but not gaudily adorned, open into the sleeping-room of her parents. This also is simply beautiful. The walls are of a delicate blue shade, and all the textures appear as if inwoven with softened sunshine. Mr. Smallfield's genius has here been brought into requisition, and he has painted beautiful groups of flitting birds over the doors. The same artist has painted boughs of apple-blossoms upon the door-panels in the boys' room. But his finest work is a frieze in Mrs. Lehmann's boudoir—for such her monogram, woven in the Persian carpet and carved in the marble mantel-piece, announces it to be—which consists of doves, swallows, and flowers in pots. Mrs. Lehmann's boudoir is on the same floor with the dining-room, from which it is separated by a charming little sitting-room. The walls of this last-named room are entirely covered with the finest Gobelin tapestry, above which a deep cornice of chased gold supports a cove, chocolated, with decoration of silver leaflets.

No wall-paper at all is used in this house. The ornamentation of the walls throughout has been put on by the hand, and generally by pouncing. Perhaps it may be well enough to state that the method of pouncing is far more expensive than that of stencilling. In pouncing, the figures to be painted on the wall are first pin-punctured on paper; this paper is then laid on the wall and beaten with bags of colored powder. When the paper is removed, each ornamental form is delicately outlined on the wall in innumerable fine points. It is then necessary that the decorative artist should trace the figures with a pencil, and afterward paint them. Stencilling, which is less costly than this by about one-third, consists simply in direct painting through perforated metal, though it is necessary in most mural work that the blank interstices so left should be painted over by hand. The latter work is, however, always more stiff than the pounced. The friezes have been painted on canvas, of course, since no gentleman would allow his possession of works by such artists as those whom Mr. Lehmann has employed to depend upon his remaining in any particular house. It is, indeed, a very significant thing that such men as Albert Moore and Smallfield should have been found ready to undertake work of this description; for, though it is a return to such work as Giotto and Michael Angelo were glad to do, we have heard of late years occasional sneers at "mere decoration." Strictly speaking, *all* art is mere decoration. There are other instances also where artists of the greatest eminence have done excellent work of this character. In the house of the Hon. Percy Wyndham, Belgrave Square, there is a grand staircase, which has on the wall, near one of its landings, five life-sized classical figures, by Sir Frederick Leighton, and at the top a deep frieze of cormorants, storks, and other wild birds; and the dining-room of the same beautiful mansion has been elegantly adorned by Mrs. Wyndham—herself an artist—aided by Mr. V. Prinsep.

The pleasure with which I have visited Mr. Lehmann's house is just a little tempered by the difficulties I have found in the effort to convey some impression of it. Passing down the stairways amid the delicate hues lighting them up at every turn, and through the door-ways curtained off from halls by rich Oriental

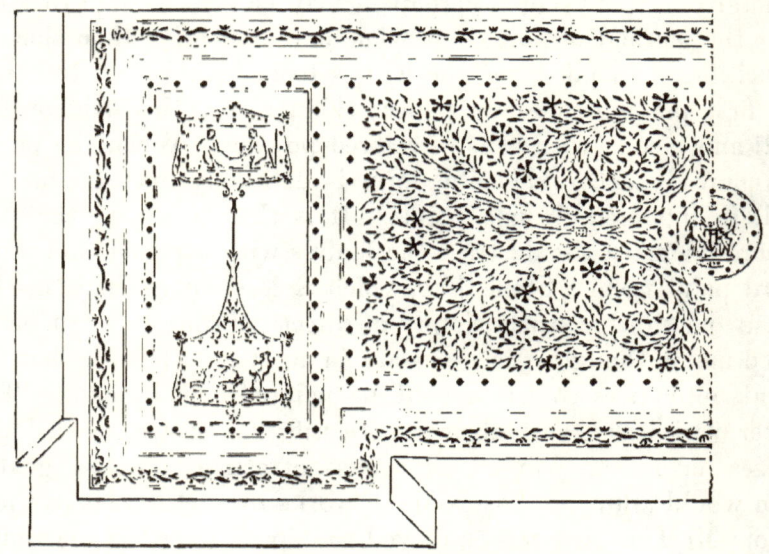

TOP OF SERVING-TABLE, MR. LEHMANN'S HOUSE.

draperies, and finding myself again in the embowered square at the front of the house, I feel conscious of an utter inability to give any reader an adequate conception of the decorations amid which I have invited him to wander in imagination. Let any one who has passed a morning in visiting the interiors of the old Venetian palaces attempt to describe them! He will have a dreamy impression of soft colors fading into each other, of apartments that have caught on their walls the tints of rosy morning and golden evening, and held them in a thousand little contrivances to catch such sunbeams, and he will feel that the subtle influences of beauty have overpowered his analysis. The finer secrets of art elude detection, much more explanation, like those of nature.

The houses I have been describing are those of millionnaires. Whatever may be thought of the large sums expended on their mansions, they do not suggest the remark made by a wit to a gentleman as remarkable for spending little as for making much, " You cannot take all this gold with you, and if you did, it would *melt*." They have preferred that their gold should be transmuted in this world, and into forms that are none the less beautiful for being costly. They are men who occupy a somewhat abnormal position even in wealthy London, and one which admits of a correspondingly rich and even grand environment. They have occasion, and are able, to have rooms which relate them to a large and cultivated world, while they can reserve for domestic privacy apartments that fulfil the want which to others is the only end of a home—a centre amid a busy and weary world for friendship, love, and repose. Even in these grand palaces one may, indeed, witness a modesty and reality which contrasts favorably with the at once stimulating and exhausting splendors of the princely dwellings of the past. There is no attempt here to heap into the rooms the great works of art which appropriately belong to the community, and should be set up in edifices built for the common benefit. One perceives, too, that the time has passed away when Madame de Guerdin could define the life of an apartment as consisting in " fires, mirrors, and carpets." The life of an apartment consists in the degree to which it subserves its end. The decoration of the *salon* may well sympathize with the gayety of festive occasions, for it does not exist for the family alone; but in the more private rooms the tired limbs will require rest on chair or couch, and equally the eye will need rest upon soft and subdued shades.

There will, however, arise in the mind of many a reader of the poor descriptions I have been able to give of these two houses (which represent an exceptional class) a moral misgiving. Is not all this a waste of money that might have been expended for greater and nobler purposes? Is not all this mere luxury and extravagance? Well, in the first place, it is difficult to draw the line between the beauty which Nature seeks as she climbs to flowers and man as he decorates his dwelling, and the luxuriousness which makes external beauty in itself an end rather than a means. Take away all that has been added to our homes by art, and we all become naked savages living in mud or log huts. But, in the second place, what about this "waste of money" so often charged against expensive decorations? Poor Zouloaga, working in a little peasant village of people poor as himself, might not have the same charge to bring against the wealthy Englishman who found him out. He and a host of artists and artisans in this and other countries might find more wisdom in Rhodora's philosophy, that

> "if eyes are made for seeing,
> Then Beauty is its own excuse for being;"

and they might add that if the taste and skill which are able to make beautiful things exist, there may be good reason why a demand should also exist for what they can supply. I do not propose to argue the vexed question of political economy concerning the degree to which luxury is justified by its distribution of capital among laborers, but it seems very clear that there can be no reason to deplore the free or even lavish expenditures of the wealthy for objects which are not in themselves pernicious.

It has been one particularly gratifying incident of the passion for decoration in this country that it has been the means of opening to women beautiful and congenial employments. Miss Jekyl, who was one of the first to take up this kind of work, attracted the attention of Sir Frederick Leighton, Madame Bodichon, and other artists by her highly artistic embroidery, and has since extended her work to *repoussé*, or ornamental brass-work—especially sconces—and many other things. She has, I hear, acquired not only distinction but wealth by her skill, some specimens of which are exhibited in the International Exhibition at South Kensington this year. There, also, may be seen the work of other ladies who have followed in her footsteps, some of the finest being by a Miss Leslie, a relative of the celebrated artist of that name. Indeed, there has now been established in Sloane Street a school for embroidery, which has succeeded in teaching and giving employment to a number of gentlewomen who had been reduced in circumstances, and whose success those who observed their contributions to the Centennial Exhibition at Philadelphia will not underestimate. Miss Philott, whose paintings have often graced the walls of exhibitions, and have gained the interest of Mr. Ruskin, has of late been painting beautiful figures and flowers on plaques, which, when the colors are burnt in by Minton, make ornaments that are eagerly sought for.

POT DESIGNED BY MISS LÉVIN.

A Miss Coleman has also gained great eminence for this kind of work. Miss Lévin has displayed much skill in designing and painting pots, plates, etc., with Greek or Pompeian figures. The painting of panels with vines, blossoming branches, and even birds, is also a pretty industry of this kind. The late Miss May Alcott was very ingenious in this kind of work, and several specimens of her art are preserved with care in England. Many of these ladies have begun by undertaking such work as this for personal friends, but have pretty generally found that the circle of those who desire such things is very large, and that their art is held in increasing esteem among cultivated people. It is even probable that the old plan which our great-grandmothers had of learning embroidery will be revived in more important forms, and be taught as something more than the accomplishment it was once thought.

It has been found, too, that artists, architects, decorators, and the numerous workmen they employ have great respect for any woman who can do anything well, which contrasts favorably with the jealousy which the efforts of that sex to find occupation in other professions appear to have aroused. One example of this is particularly striking. A good many years ago I heard of a young lady of high position who was making almost desperate efforts to win her way into the medical profession. She had taken a room near one of the largest hospitals in London, to which she was not openly admitted, that she might study cases of disease or injury, but where, through the generosity of certain physicians, she was able, as it were, to pick up such crumbs of information as might fall from the table of the male students. By dint of her perseverance means of information and study increased. I visited her room near the hospital, and found this young lady surrounded by specimens such as are conventionally supposed to bring fainting-fits on any person of that sex at sight. I found that, being excluded from the usual medical and surgical schools, she had been compelled to employ lecturers to teach her alone. Fortunately she had the means of doing this, but it amounted to her establishing a medical college, of which she was the only student. That lady is now known as Dr. Elizabeth Garrett-Anderson, an eminent physician, who has done not her sex alone but this entire community a great benefit, by showing that a woman's professional success is not inconsistent with her being a devoted and happy wife and mother. By the side of the long struggle through which she had to go to obtain her present position—a struggle in which many a woman with less means and courage has succumbed—I am able to place the experience of her younger sister and of her cousin, Agnes and Rhoda Garrett, who have entered into a partnership as decorative artists.

These young ladies, it may be premised, have by no means been driven to their undertaking by the necessity of earning a livelihood. They belong to an old family of high position, and are as attractive ladies as one is likely to meet in the best society of London. But, like the better-known ladies in the same family, Dr. Garrett-Anderson and Mrs. Professor Fawcett, they are thinkers, and they have arrived at conclusions concerning the duties and rights of their sex which forbid them to emulate the butterflies. A few years ago, when the decorative work of such firms as Messrs. Morris & Co. began to attract general attention, it appeared to them that it offered opportunities for employment suitable to women. They determined to go through a regular apprenticeship; and though they were met by looks of surprise, they were not met with any incivility. One gentleman allowed them to occupy a room at his offices, where they might pick up what knowledge they could in the art of glass-painting, and here they awaited farther opportunity. The architect who had been connected with this glass-staining firm separated from it, and, having begun a business of his own, accepted the application of the Misses Garrett to become his apprentices. They were formally articled for eighteen months, during which they punctually fulfilled their engagement, working from ten to five each day. Of course there were good stories told about them. Some friend, calling upon them, reported that, though the interview was interesting, the ladies could not be seen, as they were up on a scaffolding, lying flat on their backs close to a ceiling which they were painting. From that invisible region their voices descended to carry on the conversation. The ladies themselves were quite able to appreciate all the good-humored chaff attending their serious aim. When their apprenticeship reached its last summer they went on a tour throughout England, sketching the interiors and furniture of the best houses, which were freely thrown open to them. They are now an independent firm, with extensive business, and have gained fame, not only by their successful decoration of many private houses, but by their admirable treatment of the new female colleges connected with the English Universities.

Mr. J. M. Brydon, of Marlborough Street, is the architect who has the honor of having had these ladies for apprentices; and these ladies assure me that during their stay there and in their work since they have met with no act of incivility. Occasionally the workmen may stare a little at the unaccustomed sight of ladies moving about with authority, but they are most respectful when they find that there is intelligence behind the authority. From a friend of these ladies I heard a significant anecdote. They directed that a certain kind of mixture with which paint is generally adulterated should not be used. When they came to look at the work they found that the mixture had been used, though it is what no untrained eye could detect. They called the painter to account, and he said he had used very little of the mixture indeed.

"That is true," said one of the ladies, "but we told you not to use a particle of it."

The painter was amazed, and at last said, "Will you be kind enough to tell me how you knew that mixture had been used?"

It is precisely this *knowledge* which everywhere secures respect. The Misses Garrett have made themselves competent decorators; they undertake the wall decorations, upholstery, furniture, embroidery, etc., as fully as any other firm.

There are many ladies employed in the new Kensington School of Embroidery, which has a branch at Belgravia, in ornamenting with needle-work stuffs for chairs, sofas, screens; and I have heard of a scheme which includes art-work for ladies' dresses. In the ancient code of Manu it is said, "A wife being gayly adorned, her whole house is embellished; but if she be destitute of ornament, all will be deprived of decoration." It is not a little curious to find the remote descendants of those whom Manu thus instructed including female dress among the concerns of decorative art. This is, indeed, theoretically done in the lectures given at South Kensington, and Charles Eastlake has interspersed some valuable hints concerning ladies' dress in his work on *Household Taste*. In this matter a quiet revolution has been for some time going on in London. It is said that the artists of England once thought of getting together and making some designs for dresses, which they would recommend to ladies; they did not do so formally, but they have certainly availed to modify very materially the costumes visible in thousands of English drawing-rooms. The "pre-Raphaelist lady," with her creamy silk, short-waisted and clinging — at once child-like and antique — was the earliest revolutionary figure in evening companies. She was followed by the Queen Anne dame, budding and great-grandmotherly, whose raiment *Punch* and theatrical Judies have been "taking off" just a little after the dame herself had transformed it into its beautiful variations. These pretty reformers have emancipated Fashion herself: there is no uniform for ladies any more. At a fashionable party lately I was unable to pick out any two ladies out of a hundred whose dresses were cut alike, and the variety of colors suggested a fancy-dress ball. Yet these colors were all of moderate shades, and Hippolyte Taine himself must have admitted that very few of them were "loud." It would not at all surprise me if the world which has so long laughed at the Englishwoman's dress should some fine evening glance into one of these modern interiors and feel as if the ladies are among the most agreeably dressed of womankind. But I must return from this digression.

The Misses Garrett appear to have an aim of especial importance in one particular. They tell me that they have recognized it as a want that a beautiful decoration should be brought within the reach of the middle-class families, who are not prepared or disposed to go to the vast expense which the very wealthy are able and willing to defray, thereby occupying the most eminent firms. They believe that with care they are able to make beautiful interiors which shall not be too costly for persons of moderate means. This can surely be done, but it can only be through a co-operation between the owners of the house and the decorators which shall make it certain that there shall be nothing superfluous. If an individual wishes a beautiful home, especially in dismal London, it is first of all necessary that he or she should clearly understand what is beautiful, and why it is desired. The decoration will then, in a sense, be put forth from within, like the foliage of a tree. In each case the external beauty will respond to an inward want, and be thus invariably an expression of a high utility. Nowhere more than in the homes of the great middle classes is there need of beauty. Their besetting fault is a conventionality which often lapses into vulgarity, and their thoughts (so-called) are apt to be commonplace. The eye is often starved for the paunch. The pressure of business sends every man engaged in it home fatigued, and yet it is only when he enters that home that his real life, his individual and affectional life, comes into play. On the exchange, in the office or shop, he has been what commerce and the world determine; he has been but perfunctory; but now he shuts the door behind him, and his *own* bit of the day is reached. What is the real requirement for this person? Does a house that furnishes him bed and board suffice him? or, which is of greater importance, does so much alone suffice others who dwell habitually in it?

Here I may mention a work of much importance by J. J. Stevenson, of the Royal Institute of British Architects, entitled *House Architecture*. It is in two volumes—the first devoted to Architecture, the second to House-planning. The general aim of this work is stated by the author, one of the ablest and most successful architects in England, in an introductory chapter from which I quote. "To build a house for one's self is an excellent education in architecture. By the time it is finished, and the owner has lived in it, he feels how much better a house he could build with the experience he has acquired, if he had to do it over again. While the work is going on his attention is called to questions he had never thought of before, which are now of the greatest interest to him. He examines the houses of his friends, and discovers features in them which he wishes, when too late, he had introduced in his own plans. The designs are altered and the cost increased. His taste in architecture and his ideas about planning are changed by his new experience; the building is too far advanced to adopt the improvements, and the house which he had hoped would be perfect is a source of trouble and disappointment. He could build another house to his mind, but to go through the experience once in a lifetime is enough for most people. To have, before commencing the building of a new house, the knowledge which the experience of building gives in some imperfect and fragmentary way at the end of the process, would save the owner trouble, expense, and after-regret. To attempt to supply this is the object of this book." An admirable book it is! There are a hundred and ninety excellent wood-cuts in it also. The entire science of lighting, warming, ventilation, drainage, materials, and construction is here clearly set forth. A man who has the means to build a house for himself, and who really wishes it to be as genuinely related to his human self as to the nautilus its shell, should study carefully this work, unless he can get a better, in which case he will be more fortunate than I have been.

But Mr. Stevenson's book does not extend to the decoration of walls after they are built. The house stands in native worth, but not yet in honor clad. There ought not to be less reality and utility in the ornamentation of a house than in its construction. In the ancient Chinese Analects we read that Kih Tsze-Shing said, "In a superior man it is only the substantial qualities which are wanted; why should we seek for ornamental accomplishments?" Tsze-Kung replied, "Ornament is as substance; substance is as ornament: the hide of a leopard stripped of its hair is like the hide of a dog stripped of its hair." It would be difficult to find in literature a finer or more philosophical statement of the deep basis of Beauty than thus comes to us from a period of near three thousand years ago, and from a race whose applications of decorative art to objects of every-day use are models for Europe. The spots of the leopard are the sum of its history; its hair is the physiognomy of its passion and power; it bears on its back the tracery of the leaf and sunshine amid which it hides, and the purpose of the universe hides with it. Transferred to floor or sofa in a room, the coat of that cat is a bit of the wild art of nature, full of warm life, purely pictorial;

more beautiful than the skin of our domesticated cats, because these have been adapted to other purposes, and reduced to an environment of less grandeur. But strip the two of their hair, and they are only larger and smaller pieces of leather, and the depilated hide of a dog is the same. All of which confirms Tsze-Kung's dictum, that ornament is substance; and it at the same time suggests the converse truth, that throughout the universe there must be substance to insure true ornament. When we ascend to the region of finer utilities—those, namely, which are intellectual, moral, spiritual, social—we discover that household art is another name for household culture. What germ in the child's mind may that picture on the wall be the appointed sunbeam to quicken? What graceful touch to unfolding character may be added by the modest tint of a room? Who can say how much falsehood and unreality have been shed through the life and influence of individuals by tinsel in the drawing-room and rags up-stairs?

Just now we are the victims of two reactions. Our ancestors made external beauty everything, and the starved inner life of man rebelled. Puritanism arose, with grim visage, turning all beautiful things to stone. From it was bequeathed us a race of artisans who had lost the sense of beauty. A reaction came, in which the passion for external beauty displayed itself in an intemperate outbreak of gaudiness and frivolity. We are sufficiently surrounded by the effects of the reaction, sustained by wealth without knowledge or taste, to make Charles Eastlake's description appropriate to ninety-nine out of every hundred English homes: "This vitiated taste pervades and infects the judgment by which we are accustomed to select and approve the objects of every-day life which we see around us. It crosses our path in the Brussels carpet of our drawing-rooms; it is about our bed in the shape of gaudy chintz; it compels us to rest on chairs and to sit at tables which are designed in accordance with the worst principles of construction, and invested with shapes confessedly unpicturesque. It sends us metal-work from Birmingham which is as vulgar in form as it is flimsy in execution.

It decorates the finest possible porcelain with the most objectionable character of ornament. It lines our walls with silly representations of vegetable life, or with a mass of uninteresting diaper. It bids us, in short, furnish our houses after the same fashion as we dress ourselves, and that is with no more sense of real beauty than if art were a dead letter. It is hardly necessary to say that this is not the opinion of the general public. In the eyes of materfamilias there is no upholstery which could possibly surpass that which the most fashionable upholsterer supplies. She believes in the elegance of window-curtains of which so many dozen yards were sent to the Duchess of ———, and concludes that the dinner-service must be perfect which is described as 'quite a novelty.'" Mr. Eastlake well says, also: "National art is not a thing which we may enclose in a gilt frame and hang upon our walls, or which can be locked up in the cabinet of a virtuoso. To be genuine and permanent, it ought to animate with the same spirit the blacksmith's forge and the sculptor's *atelier*, the painter's studio and the haberdasher's shop." Under the influence of such scornful words as these, persons of taste and culture have risen in reaction against the reaction, and the result is that there are now in London several thousands of homes which have filled themselves with those old shreds of beauty which Puritanism cast to the winds. Most of these are the homes of artists or virtuosi, and, as they have thus set the fashion, a still larger number have tried to follow them. A genuinely old thing is competed for furiously; and as it is apt to go with the longest purse rather than the finest taste, we find the past as often re-appearing in a domestic curiosity-shop as in a beautiful interior.

Now, Puritanism in its day was one of the useful things, and if we do not see the traces of beauty which it has left, the fault is in our own eyes. The artists know very well that if it had spared the old furniture for the main uses of our present society, the effect would be as unlovely as if our homes were all buttressed and turreted in feudal style. Feudalism and Puritanism have alike left to us just as much of the styles of their ages as we need—enough to give, as it were, a fair fringe to the appropriate vestment of to-day. A house made up of antiquarian objects is a show-room, a museum, but not a home. We have fallen upon an age when cultured people know that external beauty is but one means to integral beauty, and when the prophets of that higher end can see that the very flowers of the field are ugly, if they drink up that which ought to turn to corn and wine. Much is to be said for the antiquarian taste, if it does not run into an antiquarian passion. It may safely be admitted that our churches need not be sombre nor our services gloomy; that a few good pictures would not harm the one, nor more poetry and music the other; but what is to be said of those who find in albs and chasubles and incense-burners the regained Paradise of man? Old lamps are not always better than new.

Much is said from time to time about the ugliness of London street architecture. I have already quoted the London *Times'* sentence about "our ugly but not altogether uncomfortable old metropolis." The ugliness is mentioned at various points of this work. But there are two kinds of it; as the famous Boston divine said there are two kinds of fools — "the natural fool, and what the carnal mind, oblivious of its duty, would call a d— fool." When Temple Bar was removed from Fleet Street because it was an impediment, the Corporation of London devoted £10,000 to putting up in the centre of the street a columnar monstrosity, carved with busts of royal personages, griffin-crowned. This is the kind of London ugliness which suggests the definition of the carnal mind. An effort was made in Parliament to get it removed; but it was too large for Madame Tussaud's "Chamber of Horrors;" and perhaps it is as well that it should remain, as the monument of that vast amount of wealth which is continually embodied in the ugliness which Puritanism made a passion in the average middle-class Englishman. But the other kind of London ugliness is represented in the miles on miles of yellow-gray and sooty, brick houses, each as much like the other as if so many miles of hollow block were chopped at regular intervals. And yet there is something so pleasant to think of in these interminable rows of brick blocks, that they are not altogether unpleasant to the eye. For they are houses of good size, comfortable houses; and their sameness, only noticeable through their vast number, means that the average of well-to-do people in London is also vast. It implies a distribution of wealth, an equality of conditions, which make the best feature of a solid civilization. There is much beauty inside these orange-tawny walls. Before any house in that league of sooty brick you may pause and say with fair security: In that house are industrious, educated people; there is good music there; and good English, French, and German literature; pictures of noble men and heroic events are on the walls; they have made there, within their mass of burnt clay, a true cosmos, where love and thought dwell with them; and between all that and a fine outside they have chosen the better part.

But, while not forgetting that the body is more than raiment, we need not forget that it can never be fairly expressed, in any but a coarse way, save through the raiment related to it. On this we must insist, that when individuality has been cultivated there should be an harmonious and organic relation between the individual and his dwelling-place. In a normal society each man would be able to build his house around him as he builds his body, and to take the past, the east, the west, for his materials as much as brick or stone. "Let us understand," says the wisest adviser of our time, "that a house should bear witness in all its economy that human culture is the end to which it is built and garnished. It stands there under the sun and moon to ends analogous and not less noble than theirs. It is not for festivity, it is not for sleep; but the pine and the oak shall gladly descend from the mountains to uphold the roof of men as faithful and necessary as themselves, to be the shelter always open to good and true persons—a hall which shines with sincerity, brows ever tranquil, and a demeanor impossible to disconcert; whose inmates know what they want; *who do not ask your house how theirs shall be kept.*"

One residence particularly has connected itself in the course of my observations with the high place given, in this extract from Emerson's chapter on *Domestic Life*, to the individuality so essential to a home, and so difficult to obtain. Those who have found delight—as who has not?—in the paintings which the American artist, Mr. George S. Boughton, A.R.A., has given to the world will not be surprised to learn that he has built up around him a home worthy of his refined taste and his delicate perception of those laws of beauty which enable it to harmonize with individual feeling without ever running into eccentricity. Boughton was one of the first to make his home harmonious with his art, and before he built West House, his present residence, he made the interior of an ordinary house, Grove Lodge, Kensington, into a residence as unique as one of those charming pictures of his which so tenderly invest the human life of to-day with the sentiment and romance of its own history. Passing once through that hall, touched everywhere with the toned light of antique beauty, to his studio, the picture just finished for the Royal Academy appeared as a natural growth out of the æsthetic atmosphere by which he was surrounded — some girls of Chaucer's time beside an old well and a cross, filling the water-bottles of pilgrims on their way, amid the spring blossoms, to the shrine of St. Thomas à Becket, "the holy, blissful martyr," at Canterbury. The embowered English landscape closed as kindly around the figures and costumes and symbols of the olden time as they do now about the features of a new age; and no less harmoniously did the ornaments and decorations of that home surround the cultured society which the young host and hostess gather to their assemblies. Although Grove Lodge is no longer the home of the Boughtons, its decorations were so instructive as well as beautiful, that I insert here an account of them.

Entering the door, we find ourselves in a square vestibule, separated from the main hall by rich and heavy curtains of greenish-blue tapestry. The walls are here, for a distance of one-third of their height from the floor, covered with a panelled wainscot, colored in harmony with the hangings. For the rest, the walls are covered with a stamped leather papering of large antique scrolls, outlined in gold. A rich light fills this little apartment by reason of the quaint and deep-hued glass of the door and side-window. In these both roundels and quarries are used. In the door there are roundels above and quarries beneath, furnishing a neat border to larger stainings, representing marguerites and clover-blossoms on a blue ground. Above the door is a curious horizontal glass mosaic, set in lead, as indeed are all the squares and circlets of both window and door, with bees and butterflies at the angles of the irregular lines. The zigzag flight of the little winged symbols of industry and pleasure required that the pieces of glass should be irregular, and this result was secured by an odd device. The decorator having come with his oblong pane of precious glass, asked how he should cut it up. The artist promptly ordered him to let it fall through some feet on the door-step, and then gather up the fragments. This was done, and as the pieces came of the fall so were they put together, with the bees and butterflies at their angles. The effect of this irregularity is very fine indeed, as setting off the precision of the patterns in the rest of the door.

Passing through the curtains, we enter a hall running about two-thirds of the depth of the house to the dining-room. The hall is lined with fine old engravings and cabinets, with here and there an old round convex mirror. The general color of the walls of the dining-room is sage-green, thus setting off finely the beautiful pictures and the many pieces of old china. There are several cabinets which have been designed by Mr. Boughton himself, and a *buffet* somewhat resembling that drawn by Charles Eastlake (Fig. 12, *Hints on Household Taste*), but improved, as I think, by being made somewhat higher, and having a small ornamental balustrade on the top shelf. And I may here say that Mr. Boughton's art has enabled him to make his many beautiful cabinets, the antique ones as well as those designed by himself, particularly attractive by introducing small paintings on the panels of their doors or drawers. These figures are generally allegorical and decorative, and are painted upon golden backgrounds. They are of rich but sober colors, and usually female figures, with flowing drapery, great care being taken that their faces shall have dignity and expression. In some cases an old cabinet has small open spaces here and there which will admit of medallion busts and heads being painted; and if care be taken that the colors shall not be too loud, and especially that the designs are not realistic, the beauty and value of the cabinet are very much enhanced. The *buffet* to which I have referred has a curtain over the arch beneath, and such an addition may be also made to a cabinet which rests upon legs with good effect as well as utility, if care be taken that the color of the curtain shall not be obtrusive.

This dining-room is lighted by a large window set back in a deep recess, curtained off from the main room with hangings of red velvet, and exquisitely environed by original designs. The window is composed of the richest quarries, holding in their centres each its different decorative flower or other natural form, and these being collectively the frame of large medallions of stained glass, representing Van Eyck, Van Orley, and the burgomaster's wife, from Van Eyck's picture in the National Gallery.

It is a notable feature of the ideas of glass decoration, and, indeed, of paper decoration, in houses where English artists have superintended the ornamentation, that realism in design is severely avoided. In this respect I cannot doubt that we are in London far more advanced in taste than those decorators of Munich, and some other Continental cities, who try to make the figures, in their glass at least, as commonplacely real as if they were painting on canvas. Even if the material with which the glass-stainer works admitted of a successful imitation of natural forms, the result could not be beautiful. No one desires roses to blossom on his window-panes, nor butterflies to settle on the glass as if it were a flower. The real purpose of the glass can never be safely forgotten in its decoration: it is to keep out the cold while admitting the light; the color is to tone the light, and prevent its being garish; and if, farther, any form is placed upon the glass, it is merely to prevent monotony by presenting an agreeable variation from mere color. But the form must be in mere outline, transparent, else it suggests an opaque body, which were a denial of the main purpose of the glass, *i. e.*, to do away with opaqueness. Even when the ornaments on the little panes are thinnest, they are hardly suited to the English sky, which sends us little superfluous light.

The drawing-room at Grove Lodge was, and that of West House is, adorned on the theory that its function is one which requires a degree of richness bordering on brilliancy, which were out of place in a study, or studio, or sitting-room. Here are to be happy assemblies of light-hearted people, in gay dresses, and the room must be in harmony with the purpose of pleasure which has brought them together; but then the drawing - room must not obtrude itself—it must not outshine their lustres or pale their colors; rather it must supply the company with an appropriate framing, and set them all in the best light. The drawing-room at Grove Lodge seemed to me a purely artistic creation of a beautiful out of a poorly constructed room. A paper of heraldic pink roses, very faint, with leaves in mottled gold, makes a frieze of one width above a wall-paper of sage-gray, which has no discernible figures at all on it. This sage-gray supplies an excellent background to the pictures—which are moderate in quantity, charming in quality—and for the picturesque ladies, who are too often fairly blanched by the upholsterer's splendor, as they might be by blue and silver lights in a theatre. At the cornice is a gold moulding and fretting, making an agreeable fringe to the canopy (as the star-spotted ceiling may be appropriately called). The ceiling is not stellated, however, with the regularity of wall-paper designs, but with stars of various magnitude and interspaces. It must be, of course, a room in which the deep tones of color preponderate which could alone make such a ceiling appropriate. In this instance it is rendered appropriate not only by the character of the hangings of the room, at once rich and subdued, and by the carpet, which Mr. Boughton had made for the room, the basis of whose design is the greensward, touched here and there with spots of red, but also by the fact that it is a double drawing-room, lighted in the daytime only at the ends, and requiring, therefore, a bright ceiling. There are two old Japanese cabinets: one is richly chased, but with nothing in relief except the gold lock-plates, and some twenty-eight hinges (themselves a decoration); the other is more complex, and has figures in relief. In addition to these there are two cabinets of unique beauty, designed by Mr. Boughton—one possessing a bevelled mirror running its whole width at the top; the other with panels, on which the artist has painted Spring and Autumn in gold.

In this residence some of the best effects were produced by the extraordinary lustre of color and quality of surface in the stuffs used for curtains, furniture-covers, and upholstery. These are such as are not ordinarily manufactured, and can be procured in London only by searching for them. Manufacturers in this country, and no doubt in America also, are in the habit of bleaching their stuffs as white as possible, and the consequence is they will not take rich and warm dyes. The secret of those Oriental stuffs upon whose surface, as they appear in our exhibitions, English manufacturers are so often seen looking with despair, is that they never bleach to whiteness anything that is to be dyed. If the Eastern dyers should put their deep colors upon a surface bleached to ghastliness, their stuffs would be as ghastly as our ordinary goods speedily become. The Oriental dyer simply leaves the natural color of the wool or cotton creamy and delicate, and the hues never turn out crude and harsh, as do those of English stuffs. This bleaching, moreover, takes the life out of a natural material, and is the reason of the superior durability of colored Oriental fabrics.

Mr. Boughton has named the grand mansion built for him on Campden Hill, "West House," in honor of Benjamin West, the first American artist who received in England honors similar to those which have been accorded himself. In this house he has had ample room to develop his ideas of decoration. It is Grove Lodge, as it were, in full flower. An excellent effect has been secured by giving to each of three large rooms, opening into each other through richly-draped door-ways, tints of their own; each is different, while harmonious with its neighbor. It would require a pamphlet to do justice to all the decorations of West House, and I must content myself with having already given an extended analysis of the ideas of ornamentation which our American Academician has done so much to diffuse. But one thing I must not omit to mention. In the removal to this house a large and magnificent old bevelled mirror was cracked irregularly across the entire surface. The eye of the artist detected in the misfortune an opportunity for a novel touch of decoration. He painted the blemish into a beauty. A beautiful vine in leaf and blossom now runs across the mirror, which, I hear, has been imitated by some who have seen it, in ignorance, perhaps, that the pretty device was suggested by a flaw. Boughton's mirror might well have an inscription beneath it from Shakspeare: "Best men are moulded out of faults."

Another American artist adorned his London residence in a way quite notable. The ancient mansion of the Lindsays (300 years old) on the northern bank of the Thames, at Chelsea, was divided up into six houses, and one of these was for some years occupied by Mr. Whistler. This gentleman's enthusiasm for Japanese and Chinese art is well known; but that large number of people who are in the habit of holding up their china plates at dinner as texts from which to descant on the strange ignorance of drawing and perspective under which the Chinese and Japanese labor, would find good reason to check their laughter should they be fortunate enough to see Mr. Whistler's rooms. The Chinese and Japanese have known for a good many centuries certain principles of art which Europeans are only beginning to recognize; one of these is, that a plate or pot is by no means the proper place for a realistic picture, but, on the contrary, that the only use of art on such an object is to give it spots of color. The chief object is not the picture, but the pot. No people know the laws of perspective better than the Chinese and the Japanese, or have greater realistic power. Mr. Whistler dots the walls and even the ceiling of his rooms with the brilliant Japanese fans which now constitute so large an element in the decoration of many beautiful rooms; but in his drawing-room there were fifteen large panels made of Japanese pictures, each about five feet by two. These pictures represent flowers of every hue, and birds of many varieties and of the richest plumage. The very lustre of nature is on every petal and on every feather; the eyes of the birds are as gems that emit light, and their tortuous necks are painted with a boldness which no European art can rival. The Japanese, when they aim at nature, have the rare courage to paint nature as it is; and, as a result, the tortuous necks of their birds tell the story of their reptilian relationship as clearly as it has been told by Professor Huxley. There are also in the room an ancient Chinese cabinet with a small pagoda designed on the top, an old Japanese cabinet of quaint construction, and several screens from the same region, altogether making one of the most beautiful rooms imaginable. Mr. Whistler did much to light up and beautify a somewhat dark staircase in his house by giving the walls a lemon tint above a dado of gold, on which he has painted butterflies such as adorn the frames of his pictures, and constitute the signature of his work. I have become convinced, however, by a visit to the beautiful house which Chambrey Townshend arranged at Wimbledon, that there can be nothing so suitable for somewhat dark corridors and staircases as a faint rose tint. In Mr. Townshend's house, however cold and cheerless the day may be, there is always a glow of morning light. This gentleman has shown that a sage-gray paper with simple small squares (such as Messrs. Marshall & Morris make) furnishes a good dado to support the light tints upon walls not papered. Where the walls are papered several gentlemen of taste have substituted for the usual dado, made of somewhat darker paper, one of matting. If the matting has a dark red stripe the effect is good, but checker marks are not pleasant. Mr. Ionides, a Greek gentleman, of London, arranged a remarkably beautiful hall and stairway in his house at Notting Hill by using a plain straw-colored matting for the continuous dado, uniting it by an ebonized chairboarding with a light-colored Morris wall-paper.

Of course tiles are sometimes used to make the dado, but either because of their common use in hotels and public buildings, or

WILLIAM MORRIS.

for some other reason, they appear with increasing rarity in private houses in any other capacity than that of adorning the fireplace. This remark does not include the use of tiles as plaques, to be hung as works of fine art—a use of them which is now frequent, and is the means of producing a great deal of beautiful work.

It is easy to understand that the house in which one resides must have a large share in determining the decorations which shall be placed in or upon it. An historic or semi-palatial mansion of the olden time will require to have its great halls and stairways and deep rooms illuminated with colors, and its large spaces intersected with pictorial screens. Mr. William B. Scott, of whose mural paintings I have already spoken, and whose occupation it is to study effects of ornamentation, has a happy field for his taste and task in his residence, Bellevue House, at Chelsea. This mansion merits particular attention, both on its own account architecturally, and for its decorations. added recently. These have been chiefly devised by the artist himself in carrying out the original plan, and add a suggestive and, properly speaking, imaginative character to the interiors. The house was built, it is said, by the Adamses, the architects of the Adelphi, in the Strand, where the Society of Arts holds its meetings (the approach to which is still called Adams Street). At that time, about a century ago, decorations in the way of carved mouldings running around door-ways, and passing all round the rooms on the surbase and dado, were in use. Previously to that time the entire walls were generally panelled, but then began the system of panelling or boarding flatly to the height of three feet only, at which

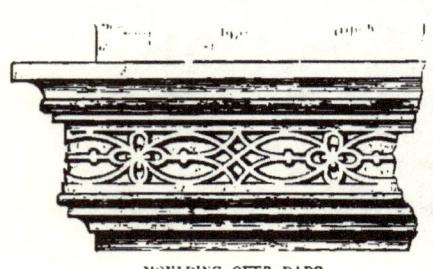

MOULDING OVER DADO.

height began the lath-and-plaster wall. Along the top edge of this dado — which, being just over the height of a chair or table, gives a very well-furnished and comfortable air to a room, and ought on that account to be again adopted—ran a more or less ornamental moulding. That mostly used in Bellevue House is carved in wood, and very good, closely resembling, indeed, those on the best specimens of Chippendale furniture, which belongs to the same date—about 1770. I may add here that the demand among artistic designers for a recurrence to the dado is shown by the increasing frequency with which a darker paper than that above, with paper cornice, is made to do duty for it.

A hundred years ago the hall of a mansion was a more important part of the plan, and more decoratively treated, than now. The entrance is here divided by folding-doors from the hall proper, which is ample enough in area to place the stair a good way back, and to give a correspondingly wide space above, on the drawing-room landing, filled in the olden time by a table, cabinet, eight-day standing clock, and other objects. The ends of the steps were carved, sometimes very elegantly. But the most ornamental feature then in use was the moulded ceiling, which was planned in ovals and spandrels, according to the shape of the room, sometimes with medallions of Cupids, and occasionally with a picture, representing an emblematic personage or some such matter, in the centre. A few of these are still to be seen in London. There is one in Knight-Rider Street, painted by Cipriani. In Bellevue House the two drawing-rooms possess very pretty arrangements of fan-shaped ornaments and delicate foliage. These are now "picked out" in colors—blue and white for the most part—producing an effect resembling that of Wedgwood ware.

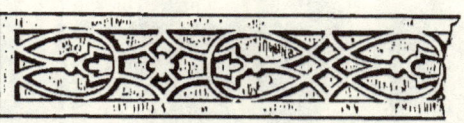

CHIPPENDALE MAHOGANY MOULDING, BELMONT HOUSE.

The plan on which the rooms of large London houses were originally arranged was *en suite*, entering one through another, connected by double doors if the walls were thick enough, so that on great occasions they could be opened throughout. On either side of the drawing-rooms at Bellevue House are smaller rooms connected in this way, one of which is at present used as a library and evening sitting-room, and, I must also add, as a room on the walls of which the ever-bourgeoning studies of the idealist take shape and color. The wood-work—that is to say, the dado, doors, etc.—is painted Indian red, with black or light yellow edgings; above this the wall is covered by a green pattern, but the upper part of this surface is divided by painting into panels two feet deep by a foot and a half wide, the *stile*, or division, between being half a foot. The ceiling is, in the centre, a very faint blue, with a darker blue meeting the cornice (two feet wide); this

DRAWING-ROOM OF BELLEVUE HOUSE.

darker blue—the blue of the sky—also fills the painted panels, which thus resemble the openings for ventilation in some Oriental countries. Across these openings a flight of vermilion birds—Virginian nightingales, plumed and winged by imagination, red being evidently chosen for bright effect against the blue—is represented. The birds reappear above the cornice, and stream in pretty migration round the ceiling, decreasing in size till they nearly disappear.

The chimney-piece of this little room is exquisite, and is much like one designed by Sir E. Landseer, which I saw among his sketches, except that the jambs were caryatides. The white marble jambs and architraves in Mr. Scott's design are diapered with leaves—laurel and ivy—of Indian red color, and above the chimney-shelf is a second chimney-piece and shelf, thus giving double accommodation for objects of ornament or use. The artist's collection of old china, majolica, and other objects of similar kind serves to render his chimney-pieces particularly beautiful. I have not seen a more attractive work of this kind than the chimney-piece in his principal drawing-room. The jambs here are panelled, the panels being filled with mirrors, and divided half-way, two feet nine from the floor, by a shelf large enough to accommodate a lamp or candle, with a teacup or other object. The arrangement is admirable both for utility and beauty. A supplementary chimney-shelf is added here, also, to the marble one; and rising nearly to the ceiling is a surface of black wood, with brackets, for the exhibition of some very fine old Hispano-Moresque ware, the golden, metallic lustre of which is favorably seen against the black. The centre is filled by Mr. Scott's own most beautiful picture of Eve, which, with a large screen covered with classical figures, sheds a glory of color through this unique room, which has, besides, the good fortune to command from its windows the finest views of the Thames.

Entirely different from either of these residences is that of Mr. George W. Smalley, the distinguished correspondent of the New York *Tribune*, in Chester Place. Birket Foster, George Boughton, W. B. Scott, and J. McNeil Whistler have naturally decorated their houses with an eye to picturesque effect; theirs are the homes of men whose daily life is consecrated to art, and a use of colors seems appropriate to their environment which might not so well accord with persons differently occupied. Those who have experienced some of the wear and tear of this busy London existence can hardly enter the door of this American gentleman without finding a sufficient justification for the growing desire of families to surround themselves with household beauty, against all the charges of the puritanical. "Thus I tread on the pride of Plato," said Socrates, as he stepped on the carpet of his famous friend. "With a pride of thy own," answered Plato, who is supposed to have got the better in this little encounter. Nature is not nowadays in such discredit as formerly for having blended beauties with utilities, making even her pease and potatoes bear graceful blossoms. And there would appear to be some reason in the tendency of her yet higher product, a home, to wear a fitting bloom as the sign of its reality. Such a suggestion is made by the subdued and delicate tints and tones which here meet the eye. One may have stepped from other houses of this fashionable neighborhood to find here a sweet surprise. There is, then, no absolute and eternal law making it compulsory to select ugly things instead of pretty things. Tinsel is not intrenched in the decalogue. Here is a hall in which gray and brown shades prevail in dado and paper, where a soft light prevails, and the garish light and the noise of the street can hardly be remembered. One may enter the nursery and find the children at play or study amid walls that bring no shams around their simplicity, no finery, but sage-gray and straw-color, setting off well their bright faces and those panels in the bookcase which tell the story of Cinderella.

To the suite of drawing-rooms every excellence must be ascribed. They consist of two large rooms and a large recess, all continuous, whose decorations adapt them to any domestic or social purpose whatever. It is an apartment in which the finest company would feel itself in an atmosphere of refinement and taste, and it is a place to lose one's self in a good book; it is a place where the mind can equally well find invitation to society or solitude. Perhaps it is the rich Persian carpet that gives such grace. It is after a pattern more than a thousand years old, but which in all that time has never repeated itself, each carpet coming forth with its own tints and shades, and in which every color is surrounded by a line which mediates between it and the next. It is not stretched up to the walls and nailed, as if its business were to conceal something, or as if it were too flimsy to lie still except by force of iron: it is as a large rug laid for comfort on the waxed parquet, which is ready to display more of its own beauty when the proper season arrives. Beginning with this rich carpet, with its sober tints, the eye ascends to the dado, to the walls, to frieze, cornice, and ceiling, and finds variation at every stage, but no break in the harmony of all. The golden tints in

LIBRARY IN BELLEVUE HOUSE.

the carpet are more fully represented in the dado, which is of an olive-golden color, with a small turquoise line on its cornice leading to the main papering. This paper is of a French tapestry pattern, in which the golden thread, which is its basis, weaves in colors that are rich but always subdued, and of every shade. There is no pattern to rivet the eye; it has no certain relation to the vegetal, or floral, or animal kingdom. This paper rises to a Moresque frieze of about one foot in depth, which holds hexagonal medallions containing the ghosts of plants. There is next a cornice of three mouldings — arabesque, Egyptian, and floral — leading to the ceiling, which is covered with paper of a rich creamy color, with very light cross-bands passing between figures in which a fertile fancy may trace the decorative symbols of earth, air, and water in an orb, a butterfly, and certain waving lines. It may be remarked here that it is only on a ceiling that any forms, even in such abstract shapes as these, are admissible. Here they are noticeable only if one is lying flat on one's back and gazing upward, in which case, especially if invalidism be the cause, some outlines of a dreamy kind are not without their value. Moreover, any designs, when raised to the ceiling, require to be larger than similar ones on the floor or line of the eye, in order that they may be at all similar in effect. The plan of covering or coloring the ceiling has a good foundation in the fact that a mere white wall overhead conveys the sorry impression that the house is left naked in every corner and spot not likely to be gazed at. The ceiling in Mr. Smalley's drawing-room exemplifies, however, one important fact: although a mere color placed on a ceiling depresses it, a good pattern has just the contrary effect. By good pattern I mean one that shows a double ground —the lower one being open work, through which a farther ground is seen. Mrs. Smalley, whose taste has been the life of the ornamentation of her house, told me that when this ceiling was being painted the decorated part appeared to rise more than a foot higher than the blank part.

The wood used in the drawing-room is ebonized, and of it are several cabinets—one displaying some fine specimens of china—bracket-shelves, and two remarkably beautiful chimney-pieces, supporting bevelled mirrors, framed with shelves which display porcelain and other ornaments. The recess which has been mentioned is what might be better understood, perhaps, if described as a bay-window. Its chief object is to hold a large window, in five contiguous sections, which admit a toned light, and have each a cluster of sunflowers at the centre. This little room has a broad divan, covered with stamped green (Utrecht) velvet, running around, and its wall is decorated with gold-tinted leather, on which are two bright tile ornaments. The large opening into this recess is adorned by two antique bronze reliefs of great beauty, and the whole is related to the drawing-rooms by an open drapery of greenish-golden curtains—a velvet of changeable lustre—uniform with the other hangings of these beautiful rooms.

It is remarkable, indeed, how much may be accomplished with rooms inferior in size to those we have been visiting by the skilful use of curtains. If a gentleman in London enters a house with the intention of decorating it in accordance with principles of art, his first work, probably, will be either to tear away doors that divide the drawing-room, and substitute a draping, or else frame it round with looped and corded drapery, which, having in itself an artistic effect, shall change the barrier into beauty. Nothing is better understood than that no square angles should divide a drawing-room, and the curtain is more graceful than any arch or architraves for that purpose. The following sketch may convey some idea of an effect which has been secured in Townsend House, Titchfield Terrace, residence of the distinguished artist Mr. Alma Tadema; though the impression can be but feeble, on account of the exquisite use he has made of the colors, which must be left to the reader's imagination, with a warning that they are as quiet as they are rich.

The question as to the best color for a wall, one of whose chief objects is to show off framed pictures, is a vexed one. Messrs. Christie & Co., the famous art auctioneers, have their rooms hung with dark green baize from floor to sky-light, and certainly the result justifies their experience; but I think any one who enters the hall of Sir F. Leighton, P.R.A., will see that there may be a more effective wall-color to set off pictures than green, not to speak of certain other effects of the latter which really put it out of the question. It is difficult to say just what the color in Sir Frederick Leighton's hall is. It is a sombre red, which at one moment seems to be toned in the direction of maroon, and at another in the direction of brown. It has been made by a very fine mingling of pigments; but the general result has been to convince me that there can be no better wall for showing off pictures, especially in a hall with a good deal of light, than this unobtrusive reddish-brown. I remember that when the Boston Theatre was first opened a wall of somewhat similar color added greatly to the brilliancy of the scenery. But there are many eyes to which this would not be a pleasing color or shade even for a hall—it would hardly be beautiful in a purely domestic room—and such will do well to try some of the many beautiful

DRAWING-ROOM IN TOWNSEND HOUSE.

shades of olive or sage-gray. Mr. W. J. Hennessy, the eminent American artist, made his house in Douro Place, before he left it for the old château in Calvados, remarkably charming by a careful use of such shades throughout. His quiet rooms were restful as they were pervaded by refinement, and each frame on the walls had a perfect relief, each picture a full glow.

The house of Sir Frederick Leighton, in Holland Park Road, is, in the first place, a remarkably interesting house architecturally, and shows plainly that Mr. George Aitchison has not only been in classic regions, but imbibed their spirit. In this house, which he has built for the artist who beyond all Academicians displays the most sensitive sympathies with various styles, there is nothing foreign, and yet the whole feeling about it is classic. The little balcony would have done for the sweet lady of Verona, and yet there is as much of Shakspeare's England in the substantial arches at the base of the wall. It is rare, indeed, that any house built in England in recent times has about it as much elegance and simplicity as this. Entering the house, the impression conveyed at once is that it is the residence of an artist. He has employed decorators, indeed, but he has watched over them, and he has secured thereby this—that there is nothing ugly in his house. A great merit! Many rooms upon which large sums have been lavished have something lugged in that makes all the rest appear vulgar or pretentious. It is a large part of the art of decoration to know what not to have in a house. In this house is also realized the truth of the old French saying, "Peu de moyens, beaucoup d'effet." For example, the doors are of deal, painted with a rich black paint; on each jamb there is at the bottom a spreading golden root, from which runs a stem with leaves; half-way up the stem ends in the profile of a sunflower in gold; another stem then passes up, ending in the full face of the sunflower, which at once crowns the foliation of the jambs, and makes a noble ornament for the capping of the door, which also has a central golden ornament. This black door, with its black jambs and its golden flowers, varied on other doors to other conventional forms, has an exceedingly rich effect. The hall also bears witness, notwithstanding its mosaic floors, marquet chairs, and the grand old stairway that runs with it to the top of the house, that the wealth of knowledge and experience has done more for it than riches of a more prosaic kind, though there has been no stint of the latter. One thing in the hall struck me as especially ingenious, and at the same time beautiful. Just opposite to the entrance from the vestibule into the hall the stair begins to ascend beyond large white pillars. Now, between the first and second of these pillars there is a little balcony, about as high above the floor as one's head. On examination it is found that this balcony is made out of an inlaid cabinet chest, the top and farther side of which have been removed to make way for cushions. These cushions have been finely embroidered with various delicate tints upon a lustrous olive satin by Miss Jekyl, and the little balcony, with pretty ornaments on it here and there, becomes a main feature of the hall. There are several other pieces of Miss Jekyl's work in the house, one of the most beautiful being a red table-cloth in the dining-room, upon which she has worked four figures of pots, whose flowers converge toward the centre. This cover is appropriate to the red color which prevails in the dining-room—a color which I do not much like in a dining-room, though here it well sets off the large ebonized and inlaid sideboard, which is adorned with a great deal of the finest Rhodian porcelain. Sir Frederick Leighton on returning from a visit to the East brought back a whole treasury of china and tiles; and he has also brought a large number of beautiful Persian tiles, with which he has made a little interior rotunda and dome which is a marvel of beauty. A sentence of the Koran runs along the cornice; stained glass throws a rich light through the room; a fountain plays in the centre. Mr. Dillon, an artist, has for some time had a studio in which every article came from Egypt, even to the inscription from the Koran (Sura 91) which makes its frieze—

"By the brightness of the sun when he shineth,
By the moon when she followeth him," etc.

Sir Frederick Leighton's chief room is his studio; it covers more than half of the whole area of the top floor of the house. The walls are hung with stuffs from many countries—tapestries, rugs, ancient Japanese silks—which all from the cornice to the floor. There are some fine ebonized bookcases and cabinets, designed by Mr. Aitchison and Sir Frederick together. The roof is arranged with sky-lights and sliding curtains of various descriptions, so that there is no kind of light or shade whatever that the artist is not able to bring upon his work. The drawing-room has a white coffered and tinted ceiling, and neat mouldings above the bay-window gather round a fine oil-picture, by Eugene Delacroix, fixed in the ceiling. It is beautiful, but I could not help feeling that some mural painting by another artist might well be substituted, and the Delacroix placed "on the line." There is suspended a very rich central candelabrum of Venetian glass in many colors. The walls are hung with cigar-tinted cloth, with modified *fleur-de-lis* spots, beneath which a floor of ash-blue is disclosed for the width of a yard between the wall and the bright Persian carpet.

In all the houses which are carefully decorated in London great use is made of tiles. The tiles which are unrivalled in the esteem of artists are the old Dutch, which consequently have been nearly all bought up. A single old Dutch tile, which when made hardly cost more than a sixpence, now finds eager purchasers at a pound. It is a singular fact that our manufacturers can imitate Persian and Egyptian tiles, but have still to send to Holland to get anything resembling the old Dutch, and even there they can obtain but an approach to the rich coloring and quaint designs of old times. Mr. Stevenson, the architect whose book has been referred to on a previous page, obtained a large number of these old tiles, which when put together formed large pictures; but several of them were wanting, and he had to make designs of what those he possessed appeared to imply were on the others. He had tiles made which, at any rate, completed the pictures; and though the new ones were carefully made, they may be easily picked out from the old. These tile pictures have been placed by Mr. Stevenson

A GRATE OF ONE HUNDRED YEARS AGO.

on the side of a sheltered entrance that leads from the street across the front-yard to his beautiful residence in Bayswater. Inside of this house there are many beautiful things, but it is chiefly remarkable for the admirable mantel-pieces on the ground-floor and that above it—in the hall common to both—which show rich old carvings set with tiles, chiefly Persian and Dutch, which are built from floor to ceiling. In the children's school-room there is a chimney-piece covered with Dutch tiles representing most quaintly all the most notable scenes in the Bible, which must be a source of endless amusement to the little ones. The finest designs for tiles which I have seen in London are those of Messrs. Morris & Co., whose pictures, however, are often so beautiful that one dislikes to see them ornamenting fireplaces. Nevertheless, the grate and its arrangements are becoming matters of serious importance in every room, and a walk through the establishment of Messrs. Boyd, in Oxford Street, will show that the "warming engineers" have not been behindhand in providing stoves, tiles, and grates that may be adapted to many varieties of decoration. These gentlemen tell me that they are continually on the watch to get hold of old grates, fenders, fire-dogs, and so forth, that were made a hundred years ago, on account of the great demand for them, and that they reproduce them continually; nevertheless they believe that they can produce a prettier grate now than could have been made in the last century. The engraving on page 198 represents a grate found in an English mansion about one hundred years ago. The one on this page represents a grate recently made for the late Baron Rothschild. The one on page 200 represents a grate and fireplace designed and made by Messrs. Boyd, which appears to me one of the most beautiful I have yet seen.

In the houses thus far described I have mentioned several which have been decorated in whole or in part by Messrs. Morris & Co., but have reserved until now a special treatment of

GRATE MADE FOR BARON ROTHSCHILD.

their style. Their decorations, apart from their undeniable beauty, derive importance from the fact that they can be adapted to the requirements of persons with moderate incomes, or to the needs of those who are prepared to pay large sums. The firm in ques-

BOYD'S GRATE.

tion—as befits a company whose head is one of the most graceful of living poets—has mastered the Wordsworthian secret of

"The eye made quiet by the power
Of harmony."

Of the many different papers with which they hang rooms, only a few have appeared to me unsuited for the purposes of a refined decoration of almost any room. One, an imitation of square trellis-work, with a bird sitting in each opening, I have seen on the walls of a bedroom (which, I suspected, might have been originally intended for a nursery; in which case I am not prepared to say that it might not have appeared in place), where it was not pleasing, and it has appeared to my eye frivolous in sitting-rooms. Nor do I altogether like their lemon-yellows, which are so well placed in corridors, to find their way (as they sometimes do) into drawing-rooms; that color, however adapted for daylight, suffers bleaching by candle or gas light. But generally their wall-papers are of beautiful grays — pearl, sage, or even darker — and, while full of repose and dignity by day, light up well under any artificial light. This firm also does the finest wall mouldings in relief that I have met with. A remarkable instance of this may be found in the Grill Room at the South Kensington Museum, to which reference has already been made. And a somewhat similar moulding is still more effectively used in the drawing-room of the Hon. Mr. Howard, in his house at Palace Gardens — a willow pattern, with buds, on a cream-colored background, which rises to a deep frieze of green. In two rooms of the same mansion the light pomegranate paper, with shut and open flowers, is used with good effect. In the dining-room the general hue is faint pink, and this is also pleasing. In the nursery there is an exceedingly beautiful paper of wild daisies on a mottled ground. Mr. Howard is not only an artist himself, but a collector of pictures and other objects of art. His walls have in a great measure been decorated with the idea of adapting them to the purpose of displaying to the best advantage the quaint old cabinets which he possesses, and the many fine pictures of pre-Raphaelist art which adorn his walls. On one of the landings of the stairway there is a fine organ, upon which Dr. Burne Jones has painted a charming picture of St. Cecilia playing on her keys. This picture sheds light and beauty around, and shows how much may be done in a house by having such objects brought into the general system of ornamentation adopted in the house. It is hardly enough to bring into the house furniture of a color which is vaguely harmonious with the wall-paper; by a little decoration even the piano, the cabinet, the book-case, may be made to repeat the theme to which the walls have risen.

Dr. Burne Jones — for Oxford has bestowed on him its D.C.L., to its own honor as much as his — has decorated a grand piano with finest art. Around its bands is told the fable of Orpheus, the potency of music, in scenes of classical, but not conventional, treatment. On the lid is a Muse leaning from an oriel of the blue sky; beneath stands a poet musing; and between them is a scroll inscribed with a bit of old French, "N'oublie pas"— motto of the family for whom the piano was made. At another end of the lid is painted amid bay-leaves the page of a book, with illuminated letters here and there, the lines being those of one of Dante's minor poems, beginning, "Fresca rosa novella." But all these beauties are surpassed when the lid is lifted. Amid the strings, which are exposed, there is a drift of roses, as if blown into little heaps at the corners by the breath of music. On the interior surface is painted a picture to be gazed on with silent admiration, for few can be the strains from those keys which will interpret the subtle sense of the picture. The only name given is *Terra Omniparens*. Between the thorns and the roses sits this most beautiful Mother, naked and not ashamed, with many babes around her. Above, beneath, around, amid the foliations they are seen—impish, cherubic, some engaged in ingenuities of mischief, others in deeds of kindliness and love. Greed, avarice, cruelty, affection, prayer, and all the varieties of these are represented by these little faces and forms. Some nestle around the Mother; one has fallen asleep on her lap. The fair Mother is serene; she is impartial as the all-nourishing, patient Earth she typifies; all the discords turn to harmonies in her eternal generation. Her impartial love waits on the good and the evil; she is one with the art that "shares with great creating Nature."

Although the hangings of Morris & Co. do not imply a lavish, but only a liberal, expenditure, they do not readily adapt themselves to a commonplace house inhabited by commonplace people. There must be thousands of these square-block houses with square boxes for rooms which would only be shamed by the individualities of their work. The majority of houses attain the final cause of their existence when the placard inscribed "To Let" may be taken down from their windows. No doubt the decorative artist might do a great deal toward breathing a soul even into such a house, if it were inhabited by a family willing to pay the price.

But there are houses built with other objects than "to let," built by or for persons of taste and culture, and to such the decorations of Messrs. Morris & Co. come as a natural drapery. Mr. Ionides, who has just entered a new house in Holland Park Villas, has shown, by adopting in it decorations similar to those of the smaller house he has left, that, after many years, the hangings of Morris & Co. still appear to him the most beautiful; and it is significant of the spirit in which he has carried out his own feeling in both cases that he has steadily refused to let the house his family had outgrown to all applicants who proposed to pull down its papers and dados, and convert the house into the normal commonplace suite of interiors. He preferred to retain for some time, at a loss, that which he and his artistic friends built up with so much pains, rather than have it pass into inappreciative hands. In the new residence of Mr. Ionides he has found a beautiful hanging for his drawing-room in a Morris paper of willow pattern, with two kinds of star-shaped blossoms, white and yellow, which harmonizes well with the outlook of the room into a conservatory. The curtains of the bay-window in the spring season are of Oriental cream-colored linen, with flowers embroidered in outline (light gold), and at wide intervals, upon them. The paper in the large dining-room is the small floral square (sage-gray) pattern of Messrs. Morris & Co., which harmonizes well with the red carpet, the pictures, and the green-golden lustres of the velvet curtains. Mr. E. Danreuther, in whose brilliant successes as interpreter of the "Music of the Future" America as well as Germany has reason for pride, has his residence in Orme Square decorated mainly with the Morris patterns. The house is quaint and old, and nothing can exceed the sympathetic feeling with which these designs harmonize with the style of the halls and rooms. It is a picture for the imagination to think of Carlyle and Sterling (who once resided here) conversing on great themes amid these quietly rich, these even poetical designs and colors. Nearest to that imaginary picture is the real one which I have seen a little way from Orme Square, namely, in the villa of the late Mr. Edward Sterling, son of the poet John Sterling, himself an artist, who had used his own excellent taste, and that of his wife (a sister of Marcus Stone), in adorning his house at Kensington. An especially fine appearance has been given to a high wall which stretches through two stories beside the stairway by changing the style and color of the (Morris) paper midway, and thus breaking the monotony. The hangings of the lower hall are dark, and the light shed down from the higher wall is thus heightened. In this, as in the majority of beautiful houses, the first effect at the entrance is that of shade. The visitor who has come from the blaze of daylight is at once invited to a kindly seclusion. Beyond the vestibule the light is reached again, but now blended with tints and forms of artistic beauty. He is no longer in the hands of brute Nature, but is being ministered to by humane thought and feeling, and gently won into that mood

> "In which the heavy and the weary weight
> Of all this unintelligible world
> Is lightened."

That mood, my reader will easily understand, cannot be secured by the papers of Morris & Co.; but where a true artist is able to find such artistic materials as theirs to work with, he is able, as in the case of Mr. Sterling, to weave them on the warp of his own mind and sentiment into a home which shall not fail to distribute its refining and happy influences to all who enter or depart.

Among the younger artists of high position and achieved fame in the fine arts who have aimed to include house decoration within their poetic domain, the most successful has been Mr. Walter Crane, who is fortunate in having a firm of skilful paper-stainers (Jeffrey & Co., of Islington) to embody his beautiful and quaint designs. Mr. Crane's "Chaucer," or "La Margarete," paper received a special medal and diploma at the Philadelphia Exhibition, and his more recent designs are not inferior. The "Margarete" paper, which takes almost any color that is not garish, has become a prime favorite among the lovers of chaste decoration in London, and the light olive tint is preferred. The daisy is the motive, taken from Chaucer:

> "As she that is of allë floures flour,
> Fulfilled of all virtue and honour,
> And ever alike fair and fresh of hue."

The burden of the daisy-song (in the "Legend of Good Women")

> "Si douce est la Margarete,"

is exquisitely blended with the pattern. The superb frieze shows, on a background of gold, the youthful God of Love holding Alcestis, the ideal wife, by the hand; next Diligence, with her spindle; Order, with hour-glass; Providence, with well-filled basket; and Hospitality, with her jar and extended cup. These figures support the roof as caryatides. Plants of alternate leaf and flower, in pots, stand between the figures and beneath the Chaucerian text: "To whom do ye owe your service? Which will you honour, tell me, I pray, this yere? The Leaf or the Flower?" In the dado are the types of purity and innocence— lilies and doves. Mr. Walter Crane's services to decorative art are well appreciated by the little folk in some households, for he has designed papers representing the most fascinating of Cinderellas and Boy Blues, and as I write is bringing out an apotheosis of Humpty Dumpty and cognate classicisms. That this artist is ambitious of canonization among the young is farther suggested by the fact that he has actually turned his hand to designing valentines, thus tempting staid persons to indulge in that kind of thing—or, at any rate, to condone it—who have long eschewed such pinky frivolities. He has designed three or four valentines only, but they have been endlessly imitated. I must not omit to mention that a great deal of the best needle-work done in London has been after Mr. Crane's designs, and also that he is at present engaged in making tiles which promise to surpass all other recent designs. These represent generally each some simple, graceful figure—classic, allegorical, or antique—with flowers surrounding them; but the charm is in the very pleasing expression this artist conveys in a few lines by his careful drawing, and also by his delicate sense of color. Whatever he does, however conventional the accessories may have to be (and they must often be such with the real artist, who will never dignify incidents with the same work as his main designs, any more than he will paint his picture-frame like his canvas), no one acquainted with his work can ever mistake the touch. When I first saw Walter Crane's papers I felt a certain heaviness of heart that one could not have them all on the walls of some favorite room—all at the same time!

Perhaps the most complete rendering of the effects at which William Morris and Burne Jones have aimed in their efforts at beautifying London households is to be found at Townsend House, to which I have before alluded. Mr. L. Alma Tadema, the finest colorist, has of course been as one of the partners of the firm so far as his own home is concerned, and the touches of his art are met with at every step in it. Passing beneath the cheery "Salve" written over the front-door, we at once meet with a significant piece of art. On each side of the rather narrow hall is a door; one leads into a parlor, the other into a library, and, as they are just opposite each other, the doors are made to open outward, and, when open, meet. Now, when it is desirable, the two doors when open make a wall across the hall; this extemporized wall has its panels painted, and thus a pretty passage is made to connect the separate rooms. One thing in Townsend House is very peculiar: the ceilings are generally covered with the same paper as the walls. There is a dado of matting with touches of color in it, or else painted in some color related to the paper but of deeper shade, and above this a uniform paper, with but slight frieze (most of the rooms being comparatively small, a deep frieze would be out of place). I confess that I have some misgivings about this continuance upon the ceiling of the wallpaper. It would certainly answer very well in rooms that were of very high pitch, for the heavier the color on a ceiling the more it is depressed to the eye. But here the sense of comfort and snugness secured — important as they are in this moist, chill climate, which often makes one willing to be folded up in a warmly lined box—is paid for by a sense of confinement. A ceiling ought not to be white nor blue, which, not to speak of the quickness with which they become black from the chandeliers,

L. ALMA TADEMA.—[FROM A BUST BY J. DALOU.]

convey the feeling of exposure to the open air, but there should be above one a lighter tint and shade, lest the effect should be that of being in a cellar. The underground effect nowhere occurs in Townsend House, because therein true artists have been at work, but one might not be so secure if the papering had been left to less judicious decorators. The corridors have the creamy pomegranate paper, which carries a cool light through them. A small back-room on the first floor has been Orientalized into a charming place by a skilful use of rugs, skins, etc., on the floor, and on the Persian divans fixed against the wall, which is covered with a silvery and pinkish paper. The chief bedroom in the house presents the novelty of walls entirely hung with a rich dark and reddish chintz, with wide stripes flowing from ceiling to floor, the effect being a grave Persian. The bed is hung and covered with the same stuff, and the lower part of each window is made into a cushioned seat of the same. The ceiling in this case is of a pearl-white, and there is plenty of light. This room appeared to me, though at first a surprise, one that was suggestive of every kind of warmth and comfort; it was, indeed, an entire room made into the appropriate environment of a bed. In another bedroom I observed how beautifully the light may be regulated by the use of double curtains, one of dark green, when darkness is desired, the other of a fine tracing-cloth, which is more snowy than the glass of an astral lamp, while it similarly softens and diffuses light.

Mr. L. Alma Tadema—a fine bust of whom by J. Dalou appeared in the Royal Academy in 1874—had contributed, as his picture of that season, an admirable representation of his own studio, with a number of his friends looking upon a work on his easel, the back of which is turned to the spectator. But one can readily imagine those friends of his dividing their attention between the picture and the rich ornamentation of the room they are in. An artist's studio is apt to be, and ought to be, as much a picture as any work of art born in it, but it hardly comes within the scope of this article to describe rooms that are expressions of individual genius and purpose; yet in every house where cultivated persons are found individual aims are found also, and there will be the effort to give to each of these its fit environment. The first point to be secured in the study, or studio, or workshop is, that everything in it shall be related to the work which is its end and *raison d'être*. When Carlyle was engaged in writing his Life of Frederick he had prepared a special study apart from his library, whose walls were covered with books and pictures of which each one, without exception, was in some way connected with the man of whom he was writing. They who are not, even for a time, specialists may nevertheless follow his example so far as to take care not to surround themselves with distracting objects. That which is beautiful in a studio may be ugly in a study. The studio of Alma Tadema sympathizes in its minutest object with the artist, who is so much at home in all the ages of art. Touches of Egypt, of Pompeii, of Greece, of Rome, blend in the decorations of his studio, as their influences are felt in his powerful works. And, indeed, throughout Townsend House there

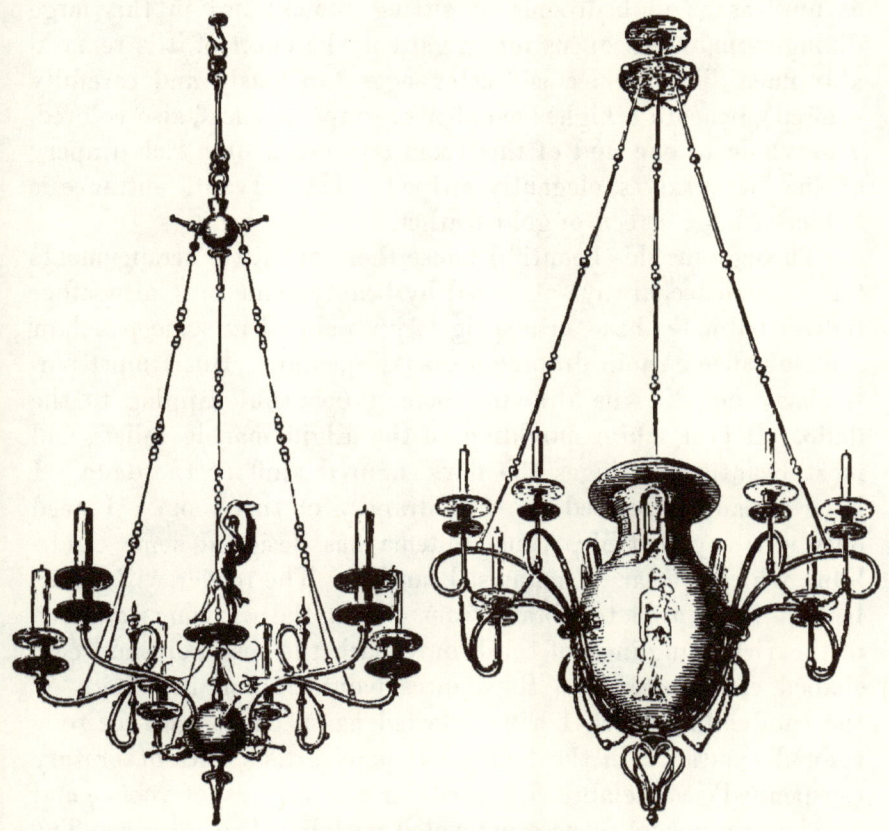

CANDELABRA, TOWNSEND HOUSE.

is a beauty derived from the fact that every ornament is subordinate to the purpose of the room which contains it. The dining-room, for instance, opens into a beautiful garden; it is, therefore, not simply an eating-room, but must in some weathers do duty as the *salon* for a garden party. The rich dado of matting is especially well placed in such a room as this, which is large and luminous. It is capped by a chair-board, which is ingeniously adorned with cockle-shells, and still more at one point with the first name of the mistress of the house painted in antique golden letters. Above this there is a cream-colored paper of squares, with roses and birds, a hanging which I have already spoken of as unpleasant in bedrooms or sitting-rooms; but in this large dining-room, which opens into a garden, the effect of it is remarkably fine. The cornice is Easter-eggs (variously and carefully colored), beneath a higher member of grape and leaf, also colored. The whole of one end of this room is covered by a rich drapery of fine Indian dyes, elegantly striped. The servants' entrance is behind a large screen of gold leather.

Throughout this beautiful house there are little arrangements for convenience, always attended by beauty, which are altogether indescribable—a head or a sprig of ivy painted in some panel, or a little gauze curtain draping a casual opening. But I must particularly note in the drawing-room a beautiful capping to the dado. It is a white moulding of the Elgin marble reliefs, and most beautifully fringes the dark-figured stuff of the dado. I have already described the fine drapery of this room. I need only now say that Mr. Alma Tadema has designed some candelabra which appear to me most beautiful. The reader will, I fear, be but little able to obtain from one of the drawings an idea of the rich minglings of the bronze with the rose porcelain egg-shaped centre-piece, and the figures painted upon it. Both of the candelabra which I have selected as specimens are for rose-colored candles. In the houses of many artists ancient oratory (suspended) candelabra are used for the centres of rooms, and also brass repoussé sconces bracketed with bevelled mirrors. The English upper classes have never been reconciled to the use of gasaliers in their drawing-rooms, and the artists have pretty generally opposed the use of gas, which is believed to be damaging to oil-pictures.

In concluding this account of the most interesting examples of decorative art with which I am acquainted in England, I add, in preference to any general observations of my own, a few extracts from very high authorities, affirming principles whose truth seems to me to be illustrated by every exterior and interior to which I have referred. The first of these quotations is the placarded principles of decorative art hung up in the school at South Kensington:

I.

1. The decorative arts arise from, and should properly be attendant upon, architecture. 2. Architecture should be the material expression of the wants, the faculties, and the sentiments of the age in which it is created. 3. Style in architecture is the peculiar form that expression takes under the influence of climate and the materials at command.

II.

METAL-WORKS, POTTERY, AND PLASTIC FORMS GENERALLY.—1. The form should be most carefully adapted to use, being studied for elegance and beauty of line as well as for capacity, strength, mobility, etc. 2. In ornamenting the construction care should be taken to preserve the general form, and to keep the decoration subservient to it by the low relief or otherwise; the ornament should be so arranged as to enhance by its lines the symmetry of the original form, and assist its constructive strength. 3. If arabesques or figures in the round are used, they should arise out of the ornamental and constructive forms, and not be merely applied. 4. All projecting parts should have careful consideration, to render them as little liable to injury as is consistent with their purpose. 5. It must ever be remembered that repose is required to give value to ornament, which in itself is secondary and not principal.

III.

CARPETS.—1. The surface of a carpet, serving as a ground to support all objects, should be quiet and negative, without strong contrast of either forms or colors. 2. The leading forms should be so disposed as to distribute the pattern over the whole floor, not pronounced either in the direction of breadth or length, all "up-and-down" treatments being erroneous. 3. The decorative forms should be flat, without shadow or relief, whether derived from ornament or direct from flowers or foliage. 4. In color the general ground should be negative, low in tone, and inclining to the tertiary hues, the leading forms of the pattern being expressed by the darker secondaries; and the primary colors, or white, if used at all, should be only in small quantity, to enhance the tertiary hues and to express the geometrical basis that rules the distribution of the forms.

IV.

PRINTED GARMENT FABRICS, MUSLINS, CALICOES, ETC.—1. The ornament should be flat, without shadow and relief. 2. If flowers, foliage, or other natural objects are the *motive*, they should not be direct imitations of nature, but conventionalized in obedience to the above rule. 3. The ornament should cover the surface either by a diaper based on some regular geometrical figure, or growing out of itself by graceful flowing curves; any arrangement that carries lines or pronounces figures in the direction of breadth is to be avoided, and the effect produced by the folding of the stuff should be carefully studied. 4. The size of the pattern should be regulated by the material for which it is intended: *small* for close, thick fabrics, such as ginghams, etc.; *larger* for fabrics of more open textures, such as muslins, baréges, etc.; largely covering the ground on delaines, and more dispersed on cotton linens.

In all the beautiful effects which I have observed the ornamentation has been in more or less accordance with the fundamental principle of these rules — namely, the subordination of decoration to use. Many persons of taste and culture have had to wage a sometimes unequal conflict with architecture whose object was a low one — to sell; but they have been rewarded just in the proportion that they have regarded the principles just quoted. It will be especially observed that realism, in the sense of exact imitations of nature, is entirely repudiated. Conventionalism, precisely because it is a degradation in human character, is a first necessity in ornamentation. The *rationale* of this is admirably given in a little book on the Oxford Museum, by Dr. Acland and Mr. Ruskin, not likely to have been seen by many American readers. The following remarks by Mr. Ruskin, taken from it, constitute my second extract:

"The highest art in all kinds is that which conveys the most truth, and the best ornamentation possible would be the painting of interior walls with frescoes by Titian, representing perfect humanity in color, and the sculpture of exterior walls by Phidias, representing perfect humanity in form. Titian and Phidias are precisely alike in their conception and treatment of nature—everlasting standards of the right. Beneath ornamentation such as men like these could bestow falls in various rank, according to its subordination to vulgar uses or inferior places, what is commonly conceived as ornamental art. The lower its office and the less tractable its material, the less of nature it should contain, until a zigzag becomes the best ornament for the hem of a robe, and a mosaic of colored glass the best design for a colored window. But all these forms of lower art are to be conventional only because they are subordinate; not because conventionalism is in itself a good or desirable thing. All right conventionalism is a wise acceptance of, and compliance with, conditions of restraint or inferiority. It may be inferiority of our knowledge or power, as in the art of a semi-savage nation, or restraint by reason of material, as in the way the glass-painter should restrict himself to transparent hue, and a sculptor deny himself the eyelash and the film of flowing hair which he cannot cut in marble. But in all cases whatever right conventionalism is either a wise acceptance of an inferior place, or a noble display of power under accepted limitation; it is not an improvement of natural form into something better or purer than Nature herself.

"Now, this great and most precious principle may be compromised in two quite opposite ways. It is compromised on one side when men suppose that the degradation of the natural form, which fits it for some subordinate place, is an improvement of it, and that a black profile on a red ground, because it is proper for a water-jug, is therefore an idealization of humanity, and nobler art than a picture by Titian. And it is compromised equally gravely on the opposite side when men refuse to submit to the limitation of material and the fitnesses of office, when they try to produce finished pictures in colored glass, or substitute the inconsiderate imitation of natural objects for the perfectness of adapted and disciplined design."

I was much struck on a recent occasion with an illustration of how little the principles thus explained by Mr. Ruskin are understood even among the learned. It was at the Anthropological Society, where archæologists, antiquarians, metallurgists, and experts of various kinds were examining a collection of specimens of the gold-work of the Ashantees. One of the leading authorities present gave it as his opinion that the specimens, though of a fineness which English workmanship could not rival, nevertheless represented a degradation of art and of civilization among the Ashantees; and the reason assigned was, that the ornamentation indicated that an original imitation of forms —some natural, others of European design—had been departed from till the significance of the forms had been lost. Of course the argument really proved a progress in art among the Ashantees, and a fine perception of the laws that must govern all work upon gold. But it is of great importance that no one should confuse conventionalism in the decorative flower or other form with conventionalism in the use of them in any house or on any object. The houses of the millions are, indeed, conventionally decorated now, and they are ugly; the individual taste will convert the commonplace forms and colors into individual expression, as his soul has previously transmuted the commonplace clay into a physiognomy like and unlike all others.

But it were a serious error to suppose that the words "conventional," "heraldic," "decorative," etc., employed to express those ornamental forms which are derived without being copied from nature, really express the significance of those forms. They do represent the spirit of nature. In the extract with which I conclude, the growth of such flowers and forms in a fairer field is most subtly described. It is from the best existing work on the genesis and evolution of the decorative arts, Mr. Scott's *History and Practice of the Fine and Ornamental Arts*, now used as a manual and official prize-book at the South Kensington School of Design:

"Taste is that faculty by which we distinguish whatever is graceful, noble, just, and lovable in the infinitely varied appearances about us, and in the works of the decorative and imitative arts. The immediate impulse in the presence of beauty is to feel and admire. When the emotion and the sentiment are strong we are compelled to imitate. We cannot make ourselves more beautiful physically than Providence has decreed, but we wish to see again, to feel again, what caused in us so vivid a pleasure; and we attempt to revive the image that charmed us, to re-create those parts or qualities in the image that we found admirable, with or without those other parts or qualities which did not touch us, but which were necessary to its existence in a conditional and transitory life. Hence a work original and peculiar to man—a work of art."

BEDFORD PARK.

VIEW FROM A BALCONY.

BEDFORD PARK.

FIVE years ago I happened to pass through Chiswick, near London, and paused near a field where Prince Rupert and his little army camped overnight, on their retreat before Hampden and his Roundheads—a scene which the perspective of time has made into an allegorical tableau of Aristocracy retreating before Yeomanry. (It is a retreat that steadily goes on still.) At that time I found it pleasant to see large and beautiful gardens, with stately poplars and every variety of fruit-tree, glorifying the acres once steeped with the bluest blood of England. Eight hundred Cavaliers were here found dead when the Roundheads came in the early morning, glowing with victory, to pitch their tents where the Cavaliers had just folded theirs. Last year I turned in to take another look at the same place. I paused again near the Rupert House—surely a very civil-seeming home for the barbaric prince whose name was twisted into "Prince Robber." Two lions couch above the projecting doorway, two child-figures stand on the ground beneath, which may be emblems of that ferocity for which the prince was famed beyond all warriors of his time, until he fell in love with the pretty actress under whose sway he became gentle as a child.

I meant to enter on the grass-covered Roman Road along which the prince retreated some seventeen centuries after the Romans made it. Here Roman coins and bits of ancient tile have been found, are still occasionally found. At any rate, it is well enough to keep one's eyes sharp upon the ground for a few hundred yards. But first another good look at the beautiful gardens which cover the camp of the Cavaliers—gardens planned and planted by Lindley, the famous horticulturist and botanist, father of the present Mr. Justice Lindley.

Angels and ministers of grace! am I dreaming? Right before me is the apparition of a little red town made up of quaintest Queen Anne houses. It is visible through the railway arch, as it might be a lunette picture projected upon a landscape. Surely my eyes are cheating me; they must have been gathering impressions of by-gone architecture along the riverside Malls, and are now turning them to visions, and building them by ideal mirage into this dream of old-time homesteads!

I was almost afraid to rub my eyes, lest the antique townlet should vanish, and crept softly along, as one expecting to surprise fairies in their retreat. But when across the Common a Metropolitan train came thundering, and the buildings did not disappear, I began to feel that they were fabrics not quite baseless. That they should be real seemed even stranger than that they should be fantasies. The old trees still stood, the poplars waved their green streamers in the summer breeze, the huge willows branched out on every side; but the turnips and pumpkins they once overhung had become æsthetic houses, and amid the flowers and fruit-trees rosy children at play had taken the place of grimy laborers. I passed beneath a medlar—who ever before heard of a medlar-tree out on a sidewalk?—on through a wide avenue of houses that differed from each other sympathetically, in pleasing competition as to which could be prettiest. Their gables sometimes fronting the street, their door-ways adorned with varied touches of taste, the windows surrounded with tinted glass, the lattices thrown open, and many comely young faces under dainty caps visible here and there, altogether impressed me with a sense of being in some enchanted land. After turning into several streets of this character, and strolling into several houses not yet inhabited, watching the decorators silently engaged upon their work, I recognized that this was the veritable land of the lotus-eaters, where they who arrive may sit them down and say, "We will return no more."

My summer ramble ended in a conviction that Bedford Park was an adequate answer to Mr. Mallock's question, "Is life worth living?" If lived at Bedford Park, decidedly yes! In one year's time an architectural design adapted to our taste and needs stood finished in brick, amid trees planted by Lindley; the last convenience was completed, the ornamentation added; and therein I now sit to write this little sketch of the prettiest and pleasantest townlet in England, while my neighbor Mr. Nash is out on the balcony sketching the trees and houses that wave and smile through my study windows. For those who dwell here the world is divided into two great classes—those who live at Bedford Park, and those who do not. Nevertheless, we of the first class are not so far removed from those of the second as not to feel for them, and to help them as well as we can to see our village, so far as it can be put on paper in white and black. It is with that compassionate feeling that Mr. Nash with his pencil and I with my pen have prepared some account and illustration of what has been done toward building a Utopia in brick and paint in the suburbs of London.

For a long time cultured taste in London for persons of moderate means had been able to express itself only on paper. Any deviation from the normal style could be achieved only by the wealthy. The Dutch have the proverb, "Nothing is cheaper than paint," but the Dutch might have discovered their mistake had they lived in London within recent years, and ventured to desire any variation from the conventional decoration of houses. Even twenty years ago the artistically decorated (modern) houses in this vast metropolis might almost be counted on one's fingers and toes, and they were the houses of millionnaires or of artists. The artists could do much of the work themselves, and the millionnaires could command special labors. But meanwhile the people who most desired beautiful homes were those of the younger generation whom the new culture had educated above the mere pursuit of riches, at the same time awakening in them refined tastes which only through riches could obtain their satisfaction. However, London is a vast place. One of the best things about it is that nearly every head, however ingeniously constructed, can find a circle of other heads to which it is related. The demand of a few expanded until its supply was at hand. Jonathan Carr, member of a family to which much of this kind of artistic activity in London is due, had become the proprietor of a hundred acres of land out here at Chiswick. It was land on which art had already been at work; a considerable part of it had been the home garden of Bedford House, where, as already said, Lindley had resided. Around the large garden were orchards and green fields. Mr. Carr believed that his land might fairly be made the site of a number of picturesque houses, both as to architecture and decoration, such as many of his acquaintances were longing for; he believed that if a considerable number of persons should contract for such houses, that kind of work which has been costly because exceptional might be much reduced; he believed also that there were architects and decorators who, out of materials sufficiently alike to be secured in large quantities, could produce a rich variety of combinations, so that a maximum of individual taste might be expressed at a minimum of cost. Mr. Carr consulted Norman Shaw on the matter; that architect encouraged the project, and agreed to devote himself personally to it. And I may say here that the speedy success of the scheme was largely due to the well-known characters of the landlord and the architect. Their enthusiasm for art, their liberality and honor, excluded all suspicion that the scheme was a money-making bubble; the slow-growing plant of confidence was already grown in their case for the kind of people who really wanted these houses. In the course of little more than five years three hundred and fifty houses have been erected. They are embowered amid trees, and surrounded by orchards; their generous gardens are well stocked with trees, flowers, and fruits, so that these houses appear as if they had been here for generations. No one could imagine that seven years ago they were all little sketches on paper, passing between landlord, architect, and house-hunters; and indeed my friend Abbey, the artist, who has visited us occasionally, says he cannot yet get it out of his head that he is walking through a water-color.

The first consideration is health. Bedford Park is naturally healthy. It is situated upon a gravel-bed, remote from the fogs of London, and with easy access to the river for its drains. Kensington is but twelve minutes nearer the centre of London than Bedford Park, yet at Kensington few afternoons between October and February can be passed without gas-light, whereas here there were only four or five occasions last fall and winter when the lights were required before evening. There are beautiful walks around, and in ten minutes by train we reach Kew Gardens. The Chiswick Horticultural Gardens are under ten minutes' walk. Near these is the long avenue, overarched by trees, the Duke's Walk; it leads to famous Chiswick House, whose sixty acres of ornamental wooded ground is the most beautiful private park in the suburbs of London, to say nothing of the charms of romance investing the old Italian villa where statesmen consulted the fair Duchess of Devonshire. There is thus no lack of breathing space. The houses are built with fourteen-inch brick walls, and without cellars. It is in conformity with what has been decided to be the prudent plan in London that underground rooms are unknown here, each house being founded on a solid bed of concrete, the floors raised sufficiently high above this to allow of full and free ventilation beneath every house.

Sanitary considerations are not neglected in the decorations. Matting is used in the lining of halls and staircases; it is easy to keep clean, and does not gather or send forth dust every time a door is opened, as is often the case with paper. Tiles are also much employed, which are also easy to keep clean; and although stained glass is used, it is as a decorative casement, and is not

DINING-ROOM IN TOWER HOUSE.

allowed to impede the light, which can never be spared in England.

What at once impresses the intelligent visitor to Bedford Park is the fact that the beauty which has been admittedly secured is not fictitious. A competent writer in the *Sporting and Dramatic News* (September 27th, 1879), speaks very truly of this feature of the new village: "We have here no unchangeable cast-iron work, but hand-wrought wooden balustrades and palings; no great sheets of plate-glass, but small panes set in frames of wood which look strong and solid, although, the windows being large, they supply ample illumination for the spacious rooms within. There is no attempt to conceal with false fronts, or stucco ornament, or unmeaning balustrades, that which is full of comfortable suggestiveness in a climate like our own —the house roof; everything is simple, honest, unpretending. Within, no clumsy imitations of one wood to conceal another, but a preserving surface of beautifully flatted paint, made handsome by judicious arrangements of color. Here brick is openly brick, and wood is openly wood, and paint is openly paint. Nothing comes in a mean, sneaking way, pretending to be that which it is not. Varnish is unknown. There is an old-world air about the place despite its newness, a strong touch of Dutch homeliness, with an air of English comfort and luxuriousness, but not a bit of the showy, artificial French stuffs which prevailed in our homes when Queen Anne was on the throne, when we imported our furniture from France, and believed in nothing which was not French."

Those who purchase or lease houses at Bedford Park are allowed the choice where their wall-papers shall be purchased, what designs shall be selected, and what colors shall be used on the wood-work. A certain amount is allotted for the decoration of the drawing-room, dining-room, and so on, and the occupants are invited to select up to that sum freely; or, if they fancy some costlier paper or decoration, the excess of price is added. As a matter of fact, a majority of the residents have used the wall-papers and designs of Morris, the draught on whose decorative works has become so serious that a branch of the Bloomsbury establishment will probably become necessary in the vicinity of Bedford Park. This natural selection of the Morris designs by so many families, independently of each other, could hardly have occurred a few years ago, or, if it had occurred, would have been a misfortune of monotony; but recently these designs have been sufficiently varied, and the new patterns, which may be had in divers colors and shades, are now so numerous that it is quite possible for all to be satisfied without a calamitous sameness. And this result is largely due to the excellent taste and ingenuity of the founder of the village, who is pretty certain to give those arranging the interiors of their houses the best advice, not unfrequently guiding them about the place, to see the effect of

QUEEN ANNE'S GARDENS.

certain papers already on walls, and showing how by new combinations of dado-paper and wall-paper, or distemper, repetitions of neighboring decorations may be avoided. The besetting sin of the new decoration—monotony—is thus measurably escaped.

The best standards, indeed, Mr. Carr is generally able to show in his own house. His taste and that of his wife have made their house beautiful. It would be difficult to find a prettier room than the dining-room, which our artist has drawn with care; but much of its beauty depends upon the soft colors and tints of its walls and its genuinely old furniture. This house, known as the Tower House, is as elegant, comfortable, and charming as need be desired even by those whose home is the seat of a continuous and liberal hospitality. The hall, landings, and rooms are all spacious and well proportioned; yet the entire building, arrangements, and decorations have probably not cost four thousand pounds.

In Mr. Nash's sketch of "Queen Anne's Gardens" the observer may see some characteristic features of the place, such as the venerable air of our trees, and the relation of our streets to the old characters traced upon the soil by the gardens which preceded these. It is said some of the streets of Boston, Massachusetts, followed the old sheep-paths; and it may now be entered in the archives of Bedford Park, against its becoming a city, that its streets and gardens have been largely decided by Dr. Lindley's trees. Some of them curve to make way for the lofty patriarchs of the estate, which we hope may long wave over us. There has been an accompanying good result, that wherever the eye looks it meets something beautiful.

One of our views is slightly utilitarian. It is taken from the

CO-OPERATIVE STORES AND TABARD INN.

old Roman Road, and from the Co-operative Stores in the foreground commands the railway, on which trains bear us to the heart of London in thirty minutes. Indeed, one can start from our little station for a voyage round the world, so many are the junctions to be reached from it. The portico of the church is visible on the right in this picture, and in the distance the steeple of Turnham Green parish church. Beside the Co-operative Stores stands the one inn of Bedford Park. It is a part of the contract of each lessee that he shall not allow any public-house (or drinking-house) to be opened on his premises, nor al-

TOWER HOUSE AND LAWN-TENNIS GROUNDS.

low any trade to be carried on upon the same. Yet there is need of an inn, that families may come to experiment on the place, and where lodgings may be obtained when houses are over-full of guests, Bedford Park being much given to hospitality. The inn is called "The Tabard." That was the name of the old inn in the Borough, near London Bridge, from which Chaucer's Canterbury Pilgrims started. The excellent artist, Mr. Rookh, whom Bedford Park is fortunate enough to have as a resident, has painted a beautiful sign for our "Tabard," representing much the same scene as our picture on one side, and on the other an old-time herald habited in a tabard.

Another of Mr. Nash's views shows our tennis lawn and Badminton floor (asphalt), which are pretty generally the scene of merry games. These beautiful grounds are at the west end of Tower House (seen on the left), and contain beautiful trees, among others the first Wellingtonia (as the English insist on naming that American institution) planted in England.

The Club is the social heart of Bedford Park, and it is speaking moderately to say it is as pure a sample of civilization as any on this planet. After claiming that, my reader need hardly be informed that in it ladies and gentlemen are on a perfect equality. Whatever distinctions are made are such as instinct and taste suggest. The ladies did not enter the billiard-room, possibly fearing that they might put too much restraint upon gentlemen who not only smoke, but sometimes like to take their coats off at the game; so there has been added a ladies' billiard-room, exquisitely panelled and papered. The wainscot is of oak which

READING AND BILLIARD ROOM, CLUB-HOUSE.

was once in a church of London City built by Sir Christopher Wren: the wood was so sound, after all those years, as to "bleed" when sawed for this room. Above this panelling there is a soft golden paper. A door opens between this and the reading-room, beyond which is the gentlemen's billiard-room. One of our two sketches made in this room looks toward this door; the other shows its great bay-window, on the seats about which ladies and gentlemen are wont to sit to read the new books with which the table is always stocked, or to take refreshments. Outside of this superb window may be seen flowers and ornamental shrubs by day, but the time selected by our artist for presenting it was somewhat after midnight, on an occasion when there were prettier flowers inside—those of the night-blooming variety, which never fail to spring up when the summons has gone forth for a fancy-dress ball.

The book-shelves, settees, and, indeed, most of the furniture in these rooms, are genuinely antique and finely carved oak of the seventeenth century; other pieces are of the dark perforated pattern formerly made in India. In the reading-room are to be found all the appliances of the Pall Mall clubs, the journals and periodicals of the world, and the newest works from the great circulating libraries. The Club has a large hall for assemblies; it is appropriately decorated, and especially rejoices in some panels, with classical subjects wrought in gold on ebony, which fill the wall space above the mantel-piece. There is a stage, with drop-scene, representing one of our streets, and appointments for theatrical representations. Here the inhabitants assemble to witness the performances of their amateur company, and to listen to concerts by their musical neighbors. Here they enjoy lectures, poetical and dramatic recitations, *tableaux vivants*, and other entertainments, at the close of which they generally dance.

Fancy-dress balls are an amusement much esteemed at Bedford Park. There is, indeed, a rumor in the adjacent town of London that the people of Bedford Park move about in fancy dress every day. And so far as the ladies are concerned it is true that many of their costumes, open-air as well as other, might

A FANCY-DRESS PARTY AT THE CLUB.

some years ago have been regarded as fancy dress, and would still cause a sensation in some Philistine quarters. At our last fancy-dress ball, some young men, having danced until five o'clock, when it was bright daylight, concluded not to go to bed at all, but went out to take a game of tennis. At eight they were still playing, but though they were in fancy costumes they did not attract much attention. The tradesmen and others moving about at that hour no doubt supposed it was only some new Bedford Park fashion. There seems to be a superstition on the Continent that fancy-dress balls must take place in the winter, and end with Mi-Carême. It does not prevail here. It was on one of the softest nights of June that we had our last ball of that character. The grounds, which in one of our pictures are seen beyond the tennis-players, were overhung with Chinese lanterns, and the sward and bushes were lit up, as it were, with many-tinted giant glow-worms. The fête-champêtre and the mirth of the ball-room went on side by side, with only a balcony and its luxurious cushions between them. Comparatively few of the ladies sought to represent any particular "character;" there were about two hundred present, and fancy costumes for both sexes were *de rigueur;* yet among all these there were few conventionally historical or allegorical characters. There was a notable absence of ambitious and costly dresses. The ladies had indulged their own tastes in design and color, largely assisted, no doubt, by the many artists which Bedford Park can boast, and the result was a most beautiful scene.

There is hardly an evening of the spring and summer when Bedford Park does not show unpurposed tableaux, which, were they visible any evening at the Opera, would be declared fine achievements of managerial art. Through the low and wide windows, on which the curtains often do not fall, the light of wax-candles comes out to mingle with the moonlight, and many are they who wend their way from the more dismal suburbs to gaze in at the happy families *en tableau,* and listen to the music stealing out on the ever-quiet air.

The new suburb which has thus come into existence swiftly, yet so quietly that the building of it has not scared the nightingale I heard yesternight nor the sky-larks singing while I write, has gone far toward the realization of some aims not its own, ideals that have hitherto failed. There is not a member of it who would not be startled, if not scandalized, at any suggestion that he or she belonged to a community largely socialistic. They would allege, with perfect truth, that they are not even acquainted with the majority of their neighbors, have their own circle of friends, and go on with their business as men and women of the world. Nevertheless, it is as certainly true that a degree in social evolution is represented by Bedford Park, and that it is in the direction of that co-operative life which animated the dreams of Père Enfantin and Saint-Simon. All society, indeed, must steadily and normally advance in that direction. For a long time there have been tendencies to put more and more of the domestic work out upon establishments which all have in common. As one baker prepares bread for many families, and one laundry washes for many, and the railway, omnibus, cab, ply for many, so other accommodations needed by all are found to be within reach of the co-operative principle; even the luxuries of life are found to be largely within reach of it. This village has been rendered possible by that principle, though it had another aim. Houses of similar architecture have in recent years been built here and there in London and other cities, but they have probably cost their owners a third more than they have cost here, because the large number of families which agreed to buy or rent houses enabled the landlord and founder of Bedford Park to make large, therefore comparatively cheap, arrangements for the supply of materials and labor, elsewhere special or exceptional. By this means one of the chief advantages of co-operation was to some extent secured. We have also our co-operative stores; our newspapers and current literature are obtained in common; we have billiard-rooms, tennis lawn, club conveniences, and entertainments to a considerable extent in common; and by the time this is read the Tabard, which has an excellent cook, may be supplying the *table d'hôte* at a rate sufficiently moderate to place a daily dinner within reach of families who may find that desirable. Thus the co-operative principle has shown its applicability to the requirements of the cultured class, who are especially interested in making for their families beautiful homes, without, as Thoreau said, sacrificing life to its means. Incomes are largely increased when they need no longer be expended on the physical appliances of comfort beyond the actual advantage derived. To keep a private carriage in order that it may be used an hour or two each day is not economy, if an equally good carriage can be hired for the hours needed. Now and then we hear a little gossip when some of the dishes at a distinguished dinner-party are suspected of having been prepared by Duclos instead of a private *chef*, but the tendency of refined society is to smile still more at large outlays for ostentation.

But while in some regards Bedford Park must be considered a socialistic village, it is almost the reverse of any community which has been so called hitherto, and is far away from the rocks on which most of them have been wrecked. No step in the planting or development of the village has been artificial, or even prescribed; each institution has appeared in response to a definite want. It was not in consequence of any original scheme that the co-operative stores, the club, or the Tabard Inn were built. The entire freedom of the village and of its inhabitants is unqualified by any theory whatever, whether social, political, or economic. It is the home of such various minds as James Sime, the biographer of Lessing and Schiller; of Bowdler Sharpe, the ornithologist (active protector of our birds); Dr. Todhunter, who has written a fine book on Shelley; Spalding, who wrote "Elizabethan Demonology;" Julian Hawthorne; Fox Bourne, author of the Life of John Locke, Miss Richardson, of the London School Board, and Miss Mary Cecil Hay, the well-known novelist. The eloquent and philanthropic chaplain of Clerkenwell Prison, Mr. Horsley, is a resident of Bedford Park. The professions are all well represented. Artists are especially numerous. The new Chiswick Art School has been erected at Bedford Park. It is connected with the Science and Art department of the government, and under the direction of E. S. Burchett and Hamilton Jackson, has already become a flourishing institution.

Bedford Park is in danger of becoming a show-place. Now and then the fair riders of Hyde Park extend afternoon exercise to enjoy a look at the new suburb. And sometimes the statesman, weary with his midnight work in Parliament or in Downing Street, finds relief in this quiet retreat. Professor Fawcett is apt to put in an appearance on Sunday afternoons, and one day the grand face of John Bright, with its white halo of silken hair, was seen among us. M. Renan, when he was delivering his Hibbert lectures, was entertained in one of our homes, and pronounced Bedford Park "une véritable utopie." He appeared quite amazed at finding in London that ideal place which French enthusiasm has often dreamed of, and which differs from the "plain living and high thinking" of the English philosophers. For here, where we have the scientific lecture one evening, we may have theatricals on the next; and if we have ambrosial poetry or classic music one day, on the next the ladies will be found attending the School for Cookery, and learning how to make dishes dainty enough to set before any gourmand. Minister Lowell has also paid us a visit, and I believe he thought Bedford Park ought to be somewhere in the neighborhood of

AN ARTIST'S STUDIO.

Harvard University. But our most memorable visitor was "H. H.," whose eyes illuminated our town for a day or two, and then went away with such pictures as can only be painted when such vision as hers comes upon such a vision as she found here. She came from a beautiful home in a beautiful land; from bright rooms decorated with many a brilliant stripe and spot contributed by the wild creatures and growths of Colorado, and touched all over with her own poetic taste; and she realized at once that she had come to sister homes with hers, where there was the same desire to cultivate beauty in harmony with nature. The brilliant letter she wrote about her visit here comes back to Bedford Park just as I write this my last page, and among the many reports that have been written of us none is more true. My distant readers will perceive that my enthusiasm is not of delusion, if I conclude my rambling paper by borrowing for a moment the pen of " H. H." " Only thirty minutes by rail from Charing Cross—gardens, country air, lanes, bits of opens where daisies grow, where fogs do not hang, and from which far horizons can be seen—is not the London prisoner lucky that can flee his jail at night, and sleep till morning in such a suburb? Lucky indeed, no matter to what sort of house he escaped, so it stood on a spot like this. But when to the opens, the clear air, lanes, and daisies, it is added that, fleeing thither, the London prisoner may sit down and rest, lie down and sleep in, and rise up and enjoy, a charming little Queen Anne house, built, colored, and decorated throughout with good taste by artists who know what souls need as well as what bodies require, there is conferred on him a double, nay, an immeasurable, benefit and unreckonable obligation."

THE END.

www.ingramcontent.com/pod-product-compliance
Lightning Source LLC
Chambersburg PA
CBHW021821230426
43669CB00008B/819